Christ Is for Us
LENT
2017

Scriptures for the Church Seasons

LENT 2017

Christ Is for Us

APRIL YAMASAKI

A Lenten Study Based on the Revised Common Lectionary

Abingdon Press / Nashville

CHRIST IS FOR US
BY APRIL YAMASAKI

A Lenten Study Based on the Revised Common Lectionary

Copyright © 2016 by Abingdon Press

ISBN-13: 9781501820557

16 17 18 19 20 21 22 23 24 25—10 9 8 7 6 5 4 3 2 1

MANUFACTURED IN THE UNITED STATES OF AMERICA

Contents

Introduction

Where I live in the Pacific Northwest, spring comes early. It's barely February when bright yellow crocuses provide the first splash of color in my garden, soon followed by velvet blue primulas and nodding bluebells. Green buds swell on winter-bare hydrangea stalks, the purple heather blooms, and by the start of Lent in mid-March, in all of its abundant glory, spring has arrived!

With these signs of new life all around me, the Lenten emphasis on repentance, suffering, and death seems rather out of place, more appropriate for the gray skies of early January than these sunny days of spring. Yet the word *Lent* itself comes from an Old English word for "spring" that was related to the word for the month of March. Perhaps the Old English climate was drearily different from my time and space, more in keeping with Lent's apparently gloomy preoccupation with suffering and death.

Maybe. Or maybe I need to reexamine my initial response and look more closely at the meaning of Lent.

After all, the Lenten reflection on repentance, suffering, and death exists not for its own sake or purpose. Instead, Lent points beyond itself to Easter, points beyond itself to life and spiritual renewal. Confession and repentance hold the promise of forgiveness and the power to live a new life in the Spirit. The suffering of Jesus—so horribly wrong and undeserved—reveals the depth of his divine-yet-human compassion, courage, and character. His gruesome death led to glorious resurrection, and the risen Christ continues to offer resurrection and new life for us today. When I look at Lent this way, I realize that Lent is really all about life. For all of its focus on repentance, suffering, and death, Lent points forward to springtime for the soul.

At the same time, I'm grateful that instead of rushing headlong toward beauty, light, and life, Lent takes seriously the reality of our world. We need confession and repentance both for the things we have done and for the things we have left undone, both for acts of injustice and for our silent complicity in them, both for pretending nothing is happening and for hoping that whatever it is will go away. Human suffering continues, and you, I, and all creation still groan under the weight of sin, still long for deliverance and wholeness. Death remains the enemy. Shakespeare aside, the winter of our discontent is not yet made glorious summer. Lent is our springtime in between the already and the not yet.

The title for this Lenten Bible study offers comfort and hope for this season: CHRIST IS FOR US.

In this season of Lent, as we reflect on Jesus' journey to the cross, we can rest assured that his life, death, and resurrection are *for* us— for the woman who anointed him; for Judas who betrayed him; for the disciples who ran; for Peter who denied him; for the priests who accused him; for Barabbas who was released in his place; for Pilate who condemned him to death; for his mother and others lamenting at the cross; for the soldiers who gambled for his clothes; for the crowds and scholars and prostitutes and tax collectors; and for all of us today whatever our age and station in life. God sent God's Son for the world as Savior, Emmanuel, God-who-is-with-us. Christ is "for" us in the sense of Christ being meant for us, sent by God's purposeful, loving will to save us and make us whole.

At the same time, Christ is *for* us in the sense of being on our side, pulling for us, rooting for us, wanting us to win. Just as I am "for" my favorite team in the Super Bowl and cheer them on, so Christ is also for us. Only, with Christ on our side, our victory is sure. His resurrection demonstrates God's victory over sin and evil, victory even over death. So Paul in Romans 8:31 asks with the confidence of faith, "If God is for us, who is against us?" Yet there is no cause for triumphalism here, for the humility of faith answers immediately, "He didn't spare his own Son, but gave him up for us all" (Romans 8:32, NIV). Victory does not come from our own striving, but is won only through God's painful, self-giving love: God's only Son given up for us all.

What's more, the life, death, and resurrection of Jesus radically redefines what it means to win. In the life of Jesus, winning looked like serving in the form of healing, teaching, preaching, and feeding the crowds. It looked like enduring the questions and criticisms of those who did not understand. It looked like riding on a humble donkey instead of a warhorse. It looked like dying on a cross. Only later did winning look like rising from the dead; and even then, some doubted or denied the resurrection of Jesus, and everyone was surprised.

So yes, Christ is on our side, and our victory is sure, if we define winning according to the kingdom of God, where winning looks like forgiveness, like suffering for the sake of righteousness, like peace instead of retaliation, like practicing faith, hope, and love. And yes, Christ came for you and me and for all the world—God's gift for us and for everyone. Christ is *for* us! Thanks be to God.

A Place to Begin

In the beginning, God created the world and saw over and over again that it was "good" (Genesis 1:4, 10, 12, 18, 21, 25, 31). Yet as we look around us today, we see that this good, beautiful world also experiences great suffering. Why should there be such evil, pain, sickness, and death in sharp contrast with the beauty of the natural world and the beauty of the human spirit? From devastating hurricanes to earthquakes, floods, and other natural disasters, with rape, torture, kidnapping, killing, abuse, oppression, war, and countless other human terrors, we might well ask: How long, O Lord, and why?

This question is at once both philosophical and personal. In theology, it's the central question of theodicy: If God is good, then why does God allow evil? This raises further questions about God's omnipotence and will, about sin and human freedom, about the definition of good and evil, and so much more. On a personal level, the question of human suffering arises from our lived experience. If God loves us, then why must we endure cancer or mental illness or any other disease? If God loves us, then why must we endure poverty, racism, oppression, and other systemic evils? Why won't God relieve our suffering? Why won't God relieve *my* suffering?

The three texts for this week address this question of suffering by grappling with the reality of sin in the world and in our own lives. They don't provide all of the answers, but they offer a place to begin by giving attention to some key questions: Is God good, and how are we to respond (Genesis 2:15; 3:1-7)? If sin is so pervasive and so much a part of the human condition, is there any way out (Romans 5:12-19)? How did Jesus deal with the temptation of sin during his earthly life, and what can we learn from him (Matthew 4:1-11)? Although the lectionary Psalm does not receive separate treatment in this chapter, it stands in the background, acknowledging the reality of sin, suffering, and the place of confession (Psalm 32).

In its own way, each of the main texts for this week proclaims that Christ is *for* us. The sin and broken relationships of Genesis wait for healing and transformation in the coming of Christ. The Gospel of Matthew gives a glimpse of how Jesus faces temptation in the wilderness, offering an example for our instruction. The Letter to the Romans brings the Old and New Testaments together in comparing and contrasting the way of Adam, which brings death, and the way of Christ, which brings life and victory.

So in this first week of Lent, as we consider weighty questions, let us hold together both the more theological issues and the more personal concerns. Let us consider each text for what it has to say, and how the texts work together. Let us be reminded that Christ is for us by his life, death, and resurrection, in his presence and power today, and in all of our tomorrows. Let us move forward with trust in God as expressed by the psalmist:

You are my secret hideout!

You protect me from trouble.

You surround me with songs of rescue! (Psalm 32:7)

THE FIRST SIN
GENESIS 2:15-17; 3:1-7

One year, I planned a "Since You Asked Me . . ." sermon series, and invited anyone in my congregation to submit ideas. To my surprise, most of the questions came from the twelve- and thirteen-year-olds: How do we know God is there? Did God intend the Bible only for Christians? If God is all-powerful, why do we need to pray? If killing is wrong, then why was David a hero for killing Goliath? What was the first sin?

To answer this last question, I turned to the first few chapters of Scripture. In Genesis 1 and 2, God appears as the great Creator and initiator of all things. In Genesis 1, God speaks and light, darkness, and all of creation springs into being. In Genesis 2, God creates man and woman as partners to care for a garden filled with good things: fertile land and fruit trees, livestock, birds, and wild animals. This was a place of abundance, for God said, "Eat your fill from all of the garden's trees" (verse 16). There was just one boundary: "But don't eat from the tree of the knowledge of good and evil, because on the day you eat from it, you will die!" (verse 17).

In Genesis 3, the man and woman do exactly what they weren't supposed to do: They eat the fruit from that one tree. Although they don't physically die in that moment, something dies in their relationship with God, with one another, and even in their own hearts. They no longer trust God as their Creator. They become fearful and want to hide (3:8). They no longer trust one another in their nakedness and vulnerability, but try to cover themselves (3:9-13). Man is no longer at peace with himself, and woman is no longer at peace with herself; for both are ashamed by what they have done and who they have become.

So what was the first sin? If we think of sin as doing something wrong, we might identify the first sin as eating the forbidden fruit from the tree of the knowledge of good and evil. But sin is more than a single wrong action. It's a more complex interaction of thinking and feeling, involving our desires and our understanding of God and of who we are. At its root, sin is broken relationship—with God, with one another, with ourselves, and with the world as God's good garden. That's the first sin, the last sin, and all the sins in between. Because whatever individual sinful acts we might point to, sin means separation from God. As we see in our text from Genesis, sin is a turning away, a refusal to listen, a rift that opens between us and our Creator.

Some might blame sin on the woman for being first to take the forbidden fruit. But since her husband joined her, others might judge him even more harshly for apparently taking the fruit without question or protest. It's remarkable what questions the text leaves unanswered. Did the serpent approach the woman first as the weaker partner? Or as the stronger partner with the most ability to influence the other? Was the serpent an actual snake like a boa constrictor or python, or was it a metaphorical snake? Was the forbidden fruit an apple? With this text, it's easy to get sidetracked by some of these details and miss the main point.

What's clear is that God is good, a God of abundant creation and abundant care, who creates man and woman as companions and gives them the creative task of caring for the garden. God commands them to eat freely of every tree except for one, and so establishes both human freedom and a healthy boundary for their own good.

Just as clearly, man and woman use their freedom to choose their own way. Instead of continuing to listen to the voice of God, they listen to the serpent's lie—"You won't die" (3:4)—and begin to doubt that God's will is for their well-being. They listen to their own interpretation of God's command—"don't eat from it, and don't touch it" (3:3)—which was far more strict than God's own word, "don't eat" (2:17). Yes, the serpent deceived them, and they may not have been fully aware of what they were doing, but they relied on their own judgment, their own desire for the beautiful fruit, with disastrous results.

The first man and the first woman committed the first sin by turning away from God.

The serpent's lie contained a kernel of truth; eating the fruit did open their eyes, and now they could see. But the truth was harsh, for they saw themselves for what they had become: not only physically naked as before, but naked in their sin, wanting to hide from God and ashamed in the presence of one another, ashamed of themselves. Their easy companionship with one another and with God had died. Sin had entered the world.

As I reflect further on my youth asking, "what was the first sin?" I'm encouraged by their curiosity and thirst for biblical knowledge. But I also know that for them and for all of us, the more immediate question is: Given the presence of sin in the world, how shall we live? In other words, how do I hear God's voice in the midst of the other voices in the world and in my own head and heart? How do I express my God-given human freedom? What are the God-given boundaries that are good for me, that help me use my freedom wisely?

In Genesis, the man and woman listened to the serpent's lie and to their human reasoning instead of listening for God's voice in their lives. Today, we may also find ourselves distracted by other voices: advertising that encourages a consumer mentality, movies that promote hyper-sexuality and violence, an economic system built on selfishness and greed, political commentary that's more adversarial than illuminating, the always-on draw of social media. Sometimes the loud and contradictory voices of our world can be deafening.

That's why I keep a weekly social media Sabbath as a healthy boundary. The 24-7 digital world offers enormous freedom where information and social contacts remain available at any time. But sometimes the information overload is just too much. So from Saturday evening to Sunday evening, I step back from the constant rush and take a social media Sabbath that reminds me to listen for God's voice both off- and on-line. Social media isn't exactly the forbidden fruit in the garden of Eden. For me, it's both fun and functional, a useful communication tool that can help maintain positive relationships. Plus I'm not always consistent with my digital Sabbath, like the time I couldn't resist checking Facebook for the announcement of a new baby in my church family. Still, I find that stepping away from social media has become a regular enough practice that I miss it when I break it, and I'm convinced it helps me listen for God's voice in the midst of the many other voices in my world.

What spiritual disciplines or other practices help you listen for God's voice? What boundaries help you deal with individualism, consumerism, and other influential voices of our culture?

BUT IT'S NOT FAIR!
ROMANS 5:12-19

I'm thankful for the Thursday night Sacred Pauses group I meet with, where we pause in the middle of a busy week to gather around Scripture, pray, and share together. Sometimes the sharing and prayer take up most or all of our evening depending on the need. But mainly we spend time journaling to music or practicing lectio divina, taking time for silent reflection, or a more traditional Bible study.

When our group first read these verses from Romans together, we weren't sure what to think. The language seemed so dense, and the concepts unfamiliar. So I brought in a large markerboard and divided it in two, with "Adam" on one side and "Christ" on the other. "Let's read through the text a second time," I said, "and let's try to put anything related to Adam on one side and anything related to Christ on the other."

Soon we had our two lists. On Adam's side: sin, death, failure, wrong, consequences of sin, judgment, punishment, disobedience. On Christ's side: the one who was coming, free gift, grace, God's grace, multiplied grace, acquittal, righteousness, life, obedience. In some cases, the words stood in opposition to one another: disobedience versus obedience, sin versus grace, wrong versus righteousness, death versus life. Adam seemed to represent one way of being and behaving in the world, and Christ represented another very different way of being and behaving.

Although the two apparently moved in opposite directions, they shared an important dynamic in that both impacted other people. In the case of Adam, one man brought unrighteousness, sin, and death to many. In the case of Christ, one man brought righteousness, grace, and life to many. Our Romans text doesn't tell us how any of that happened, but clearly, both Adam and Christ made a tremendous impact on the lives of other people. Just as clearly, the effect of Christ was greater than the effect of Adam. For in Christ, God multiplied grace upon grace to far outweigh Adam's sin. The righteousness of Christ undid Adam's wrong. Life in Christ surpassed the death brought by Adam.

As our group continued to compare and contrast the two lists on our markerboard, the argument in our text from Romans began to make more sense. The power of sin affects us and every human being because of Adam. Sin, suffering, and death, are embedded in human life—whether as part of human biology, or imprinted as some kind of spiritual DNA, or as a product of our inevitably wrong choices in life, or by some other means. We may not know precisely *how* from our text, but we know what: Since Adam, sin has become a universal human problem.

It hardly seems fair that Adam's sin should have ruined things for all of us. Why should that be so, and how could it even be possible? But equally so, it isn't fair that Jesus' death should bring grace for everyone. But that seems to be the point of our text. In fact, says Romans, the grace of God is even greater than the effects of Adam's sin. The way out of sin is not through our own striving or good works. We can't escape the inescapable. But release from the power of sin and death comes through the work of Christ, which is the free gift of God. If sin is a universal human problem, Christ is the ultra-universal answer. No, it's not fair. It's even better than fair, for it's God's grace.

Between the two columns on our markerboard, I drew a series of greater than signs to show that Christ is greater than Adam, life is greater than death, righteousness greater than wrong, obedience greater than disobedience. Yet we still had a gap in our understanding of our text. Romans 5:14 says that "death ruled from Adam until Moses," and verse 15 says that God's grace came in the person of Jesus Christ. That definitely rated a greater than sign. But what of the time between Moses and Christ? How are we to understand that part of our theological timeline?

Our text contains just one brief reference to the Law in verse 13, followed by the reference to Moses in verse 14. The first readers of Romans would have readily put these two together, for they would have known that Moses received the Ten Commandments at Mount Sinai (Exodus 20:1-17), and these were followed by other commandments and instructions given by God. Together, these made up the Law, which functioned to highlight the reality of sin and to draw some healthy boundaries for the Israelite community. So if death reigned from Adam to Moses, we might say that the Law "reigned" from Moses to Christ. The apostle Paul expands on this view in the Book of Galatians, where he calls the Law "a custodian until Christ" (Galatians 3:24).

Our Thursday night group had an engaging and enjoyable discussion, and we now had a good working knowledge of the theology of our text. I even took a picture of our markerboard that night for future reference. But what did all of that good theology have to do with us? Was there more to our text than that? Besides stretching our philosophical and theological muscles, what practical application could these verses have for us today?

As we pondered the two contrasting legacies of Adam and Christ, we realized that they represented more than sound theology. They also offered some practical, down-to-earth encouragement for daily living. When sin and suffering appear to have the upper hand in our world, this text reminds us that the grace and gift of God are far greater. When we are sick of death with too many homeless youths on the street and too many wars in the world, we can know that the way of Christ points away from wrong to righteousness, away from death to new life and hope. When we struggle with personal temptations and failures, we can know that they are not the end, that our legacy from

Adam pales in comparison to the legacy of grace and forgiveness in Jesus Christ.

For all the big ideas in these verses, they also nurture a deeply personal sense of God's grace. If sin is so universal and so pervasive, if there is no way out by our own will or power, then how much more do we need God's forgiveness, and how much more will God shower us with grace. Thankfully for us, God doesn't insist on playing "fair." Instead, God multiplied grace in Jesus Christ to far surpass Adam's sin, the sin of the world, and our own.

In what ways do you feel the weight of sin in the world and in your own life? Where do you see signs of God's surpassing grace?

JUST SAY NO
MATTHEW 4:1-11

The Devil

The Greek word for temptation means testing or trial. So when we're tempted to take all the credit for a team effort, when we're tempted to respond insult for insult in an argument, when we're tempted to cut an ethical corner or two behind the scenes to look good up front—we might think of these as tests of character, as trials that reveal who we really are. That's the kind of temptation, testing, and trial that Jesus also faces in the wilderness. *Character is revealed in times of crisis*

In the first trial, the devil tempts Jesus to turn stones into bread. Jesus had already been in the wilderness fasting for forty days, so surely he was now entitled to eat. Why not turn stones into bread to satisfy his hunger? What could be wrong with that? But temptation is not always between right and wrong, between good and bad; the test of character may be focused instead on doing something good for the wrong reason or at the wrong time. The day would come when Jesus would eat, and another day would come when he would even multiply bread and fish to feed a crowd (Matthew 14:13-21). But in this instance, he chooses not to use divine power to satisfy himself on the devil's say-so. Instead, Jesus insists on waiting for God's word in God's time.

For a second trial, the devil does not deny that Jesus is the Son of God, but tests him exactly on that point. What will Jesus do as the Son of God? Will he use God's power to draw attention to himself, to attract followers by having God perform a miracle? Again, the time would come when Jesus would perform many signs and wonders—he would calm storms, cast out demons, heal the sick, and even raise the dead—but not for public acclaim or approval, not for money or personal gain. In fact, Jesus often told people to be quiet about their miraculous experiences. His miracles were not advertising, but signs of God's kingdom meant to bring justice and hope, salvation, and peace. Here in the wilderness, Jesus refuses to play the devil's game of testing God.

Finally, the devil takes Jesus to a high mountain and offers him all the kingdoms of the world in return for his allegiance in worship. Think of all the good that Jesus could do if he had all that power. He could rid the world of political corruption, poverty, slavery, war, and every kind of oppression. Once again, Jesus refuses to give in to temptation. One day his authority over all things would become clear, but only after his own suffering and brutal death, only after his resurrection, ascension, and coming again. In the meantime, he would not take the devil's shortcut.

Three separate trials, three separate victories—and yet each temptation was really a variation on the same theme. In the first instance, Jesus faced the temptation to doubt God's provision and look out for his own needs. In the second, he faced the temptation to doubt God's faithfulness and seek the approval of other people. In the last, he faced the temptation to doubt God's power and take the easy way to glory. Just as the serpent tempted the first man and first woman to doubt God's word and turn away, so the devil tempts Jesus at the same critical point.

Sound familiar? We may not have the power to turn stones into bread, but we may also be tempted to doubt God's provision and try to get what we want in our own way and in our own time. We may not test God by throwing ourselves off a building, but we might be tempted to misuse God's power for our own ends or to please other people. When we're faced with challenges, we may find ourselves tempted to take the easy way out instead of relying on God's strength and leading to see us through. We, too, know the temptation of doubting God and turning away.

Jesus shows us a more faithful, God-honoring way.

From Jesus' example, when we're tested, we can learn to say no to temptation with Scripture. Of course, quoting Scripture is no guarantee that we've got it right. In our text, the devil misuses Scripture to tempt Jesus, and we know that Scripture has been misused throughout history and even today to justify racism, oppression, war, and other forms of injustice. But the misuse of Scripture gives us even more reason to read carefully and to study, to immerse ourselves in the Word as Jesus did, to know it deeply as our guide for life and faith.

We can also learn from Jesus' example to say no to temptation by remembering who and whose we are. Just before his temptation in the wilderness, Jesus had been baptized by John, and the Spirit of God descended on him like a dove. Divine confirmation came as a voice from heaven saying, "This is my Son whom I dearly love; I find happiness in him" (Matthew 3:17). As the beloved Son, Jesus faced temptation empowered by the Spirit and knowing who and whose he was. Remembering who we are as precious children of God also strengthens us in the face of temptation. We are created in God's image, empowered by the Spirit to bear that image of God into our world and into the challenges we face each day.

From Jesus we also learn to say no to temptation by putting God first. We are not to worship money or success, convenience or consumerism, or any other idol. Even the good things of life—family, church, work, community service, and every other good thing—find their best place in our lives in light of God's kingdom. When we say yes to God first, other things take their rightful place, and the noes we need to say become more obvious. As Jesus dismisses the devil, his words also challenge our priorities today: "You will worship the Lord your God and serve only him" (verse 10).

In Genesis, the serpent tests the first man and woman, and they fail miserably as they commit the first sin. Here in the Gospel of Matthew, the devil tests Jesus three times, and Jesus surpasses every test. Empowered by the Spirit, grounded in Scripture, knowing who and whose he was, placing his full trust in God, Jesus overcame every temptation. As we face temptation, testing, and trial in our lives today, God sets the same path before us.

Which temptation stands out as the most challenging for you today: to put your own needs first, to please others, or to take the easy way out? What helps you to say no?

Psalm 32

¹ The one whose wrongdoing is forgiven,
  whose sin is covered over, is truly happy!
² The one the LORD doesn't consider guilty—
  in whose spirit there is no dishonesty—
  that one is truly happy!
³ When I kept quiet, my bones wore out;
  I was groaning all day long—
  every day, every night!—
⁴ because your hand was heavy upon me.
  My energy was sapped as if in a summer drought.
⁵ So I admitted my sin to you;
  I didn't conceal my guilt.
  "I'll confess my sins to the LORD," is what I said.
  Then you removed the guilt of my sin.
⁶ That's why all the faithful should pray to you during troubled times,
  so that a great flood of water won't reach them.
⁷ You are my secret hideout!
  You protect me from trouble.
  You surround me with songs of rescue!
⁸ I will instruct you and teach you
  about the direction you should go.
  I'll advise you and keep my eye on you.
⁹ Don't be like some senseless horse or mule,
  whose movement must be controlled with a bit and a bridle.
   Don't be anything like that!
¹⁰ The pain of the wicked is severe,
  but faithful love surrounds the one who trusts the LORD.
¹¹ You who are righteous, rejoice in the LORD and be glad!
  All you whose hearts are right, sing out in joy!

GROUP STUDY GUIDE

Questions for Discussion

1. Giving up something for Lent is one concrete way to reflect on the sacrifice of Jesus as we walk through this season. For some, that might mean fasting from coffee, chocolate, fast-food, television, listening to sports news, checking social media, or another regular habit. Some might choose something less physical but just as personal, like fasting from foul language or fasting from worry. While these may seem trivial compared to the suffering and death of Jesus, even such small sacrifices can serve as consistent reminders. Do you normally give up something for Lent? Why or why not?

2. If you've chosen to give up something for Lent, share it with the group and tell them why this practice has meaning for you. If not, consider choosing something. Even though Lent has already begun, it's not too late to join in.

3. Review Genesis 2:15-17; 3:1-7. At what point did temptation turn into sin for the first man and woman? How can you tell the difference between temptation and sin in your life?

4. Romans 5:12-19 speaks of sin as a singular power that ushered in death, but in the Bible sin also seems to take the form of individual sins, as in Exodus 20:1-17; Matthew 5:17-20; Ephesians 4:31; and elsewhere. What is the significance of emphasizing sin as a power and sin as individual acts?

5. In Matthew 4:1-11, Jesus answers each temptation with Scripture. Which verses of Scripture help you to establish good priorities and to say no to temptation?

Suggestions for Group Study

Confront Temptation

Brainstorm a list of everyday temptations (gossip, overeating, speeding, viewing inappropriate material online, and so forth). Then choose one and develop practical strategies for addressing it. Include both negative strategies (for example, ways of saying no) and positive strategies (for example, things to do instead).

Write a Prayer of Confession

As part of corporate worship, prayers of confession and words of assurance remind us that authentic relationship with God means being honest about who we are and who God is. In humility, we confess our humanity, our limitations, our shortcomings and failures, and we receive the assurance of God's love and pardon. Confession and assurance go together like two sides of the same coin.

For a personal or group activity, write a prayer of confession and words of assurance. Try it freestyle if you wish, or use the outline below. For a personal activity in a group setting, you may wish to play some music while each person works alone for a time. Then allow opportunity for everyone to share their prayer if they choose, while making it clear that sharing is entirely optional. To write a prayer as a group, use a large markerboard and give everyone an opportunity to contribute as they choose.

a. Begin by addressing God in a way that acknowledges God's holiness and mercy.

b. Describe your thoughts and feelings as you approach God—are you coming in humility, remorse, anger, faith, dependence on God, or something else?

c. Make your confession. For a personal prayer, reflect on your inner life of thoughts, feelings, and motivations, as well as your outward actions and how you engage with others. For a group prayer, reflect on the needs of the group and expand that to include your community and world.

d. For words of assurance, consider including or adapting words from Psalm 32:1-2; Psalm 103:8-12; 2 Corinthians 5:17; Ephesians 1:7-8; Colossians 1:13-14; 1 John 1:8-9.

Closing Prayer

When we ignore the power of sin, when we refuse to recognize any of our wrongs, we fail at being authentic with ourselves and with others, with the world around us, and most of all with you, O God of love and mercy. Forgive us our failures. Bring us into your light and truth, that we may turn to you and be set free from any falsehood or fear. Empower us by your Spirit, that we may know your forgiveness in Jesus Christ and live inspired and led by your Word. Amen.

Faith for the Journey

When quarterback Tim Tebow played college football for the Florida Gators, he won a Heisman Trophy as the most valuable player in American college football. The following year, when he wrote John 3:16 on his eye black for a collegiate national championship game, for the next twenty-four hours that one verse became the highest ranked search on Google. John 3:16 frequently appears in public in other ways as well. A chain of fashion stores stamps John 3:16 on the bottom of each shopping bag. A California fast-food outlet prints John 3:16 on the inside bottom rim of each beverage cup, and other Bible references on each bag of fries.

Are these creative ways of sharing faith? Or do they turn people off? Are they effective forms of testimony if they make people curious, at least enough to look up a verse reference on Google? Or is it disrespectful to put a verse of Scripture on a paper cup or bag that's going to get crumpled up, recycled, or thrown in the trash? Is it misleading to cite just one verse out of context? Is it a kind of fast-food, fast-fashion treatment of Scripture when what we really need today is deep reflection and engagement?

This week, the story of Abram portrays faith in action as he sets out on a new journey with new challenges and new blessings ahead. The Letter to the Romans further reflects on Abram's faith and its implications for all who believe. His faith meant transformation, symbolized by his subsequent name change from Abram to Abraham (Genesis 17:5), and faith continues to mean transformation, challenge, and blessing for all of us today. In the Gospel of John, Nicodemus experiences a faith journey of his own—not one of traveling to a foreign land, but a journey of heart and mind as he talks with Jesus and discovers the meaning of new birth. The words of the psalmist apply to Abram/ Abraham, Nicodemus, and to all of us: "The LORD will protect you on your journeys—whether going or coming—from now until forever from now" (Psalm 121:8).

These texts offer a more robust view of faith than painting a Scripture reference on your face or printing it on a paper bag. But might there also be a place for such public gestures? If they remain the sole content of our witness, then clearly they don't go far enough. But if John 3:16 at a sporting event arouses curiosity about Scripture, might that be a good thing especially in an age where biblical illiteracy seems on the rise? If a Scripture reference on a bag of fries can provoke questions about the nature and relevancy of faith, then why not include it? If such public gestures provide opportunity for further testimony, if they are backed up by Christian character, worship, and faithful living in service, peace, and justice, perhaps they might also pave the way for deep and genuine faith.

A JOURNEY OF BLESSING
GENESIS 12:1-4a

Before I sat down to write this reflection, I checked my Twitter feed and came across verse 3 of this text as a PowerPoint slide by Logos Bible Software. How wonderful to see it as the Logos Verse of the Day, since I had already begun mulling it over as one of my verses for the day too. On the PowerPoint slide, Abram appears in the center as a stylized bright blue figure, flanked by other gray and less distinct figures stretching out in the darkness on either side and standing along the curve of the earth. The slide makes an apt visual interpretation of the last part of the verse: "All the families of the earth will be blessed because of you" (Genesis 12:3).

In many ways, Abram stands as the central figure of our text as suggested by the Logos slide. Abram hears God's command to leave his familiar surroundings and set out for an unknown land. He receives God's promise to make him a great nation, a great man, and a great blessing to others. What's more, he follows through on all that he has heard, for he goes "just as the LORD told him" (verse 4). With the exception of a side reference to his nephew, Lot, Abram appears alone as the main character of his story.

That, at least, is the way it might appear; however, just as in the opening chapters of Genesis, so here in our text, God is the great Initiator. God chooses Abram and tells him to "go." God promises to turn him into a respected man and a great nation. God widens Abram's promised blessing to include his whole family and the whole world. It is not Abram, but God who initiates the spirit of adventure and who envisions all that will unfold. This may be Abram's story, but even more, this is God's story.

Years ago, when my husband and I moved from our home in British Columbia, Canada, to seminary in Indiana, we felt called by God and excited to experience a new setting, to learn new things, and to meet new people. Yet we also went with a sense of loss as we left behind our familiar surroundings for the unfamiliar. We went from being citizens in our own country to living as resident aliens in a foreign land; exchanging the waterfront and the mountains of home for the endless Midwest prairie; leaving behind our family and the church we loved to make our way among strangers.

I imagine that was part of Abram's story too. He left his land and his father's household for a new land among new people. How exciting for him to hear God's call and venture out in faith! Yet also how difficult, strange, and full of loss. Starting over at the age of seventy-five would have been difficult, especially in a traditional culture unused to the mobility of our day. Traveling through the desert meant physical danger and uncertainty. He and his wife, Sarai, faced famine, living as new immigrants in Egypt, fearing for their lives, moving on once again— and that's just their story in Genesis 12. More challenges awaited them as their story continued, and as God's purposes continued to unfold.

Our text is clear that God's intention was not only for Abram and his family, but for all the families of the earth. Just as everything made in creation was "supremely good" (Genesis 1:31), so we might use the same words to describe God's intention in our text. God envisioned something "supremely good," with blessing for Abram's family and all families. Abram and Sarai would become Abraham and Sarah; they would have a son; their descendants would become a great people; and one day from their lineage, Jesus would be born as Savior and

King, bringing the blessing of God's presence, forgiveness, and peace to all. Abram and Sarai couldn't have known all of that, but as they faced many challenges on their journey, I imagine them returning again and again to God's words of blessing. God would not abandon them in the desert, for there was blessing ahead.

When the cold of our first prairie winter made my husband and me long for the milder weather back home, whenever we felt lonely or grumpy or discouraged, we reminded ourselves of God's call in our lives. God had started us on this journey to seminary and would not abandon us. There was blessing for us too, in the joy of studying and learning many new things; in our cozy student apartment; in making new friends; and in getting to know a new church and a new community. We could also offer God's blessing to others. Not to all of the families of the world, but to the people we met face to face in the course of daily living: to the student families who shared our row of housing, to students from Germany, Nigeria, and elsewhere who were even further from home than we were. By faith, we, too, lived and journeyed in the tradition of Abraham and Sarah.

Today, my husband and I are still on a journey, although we're now settled back in Canada and have no plans for relocating any time soon. All of us are on a journey through life, and God goes with us. Whether it's crossing the border to another country or crossing the street in our hometown—changing schools, changing jobs, volunteering for something new in our church or community, facing illness or the loss of a loved one, or whatever other challenges life brings—we can move forward knowing that God will not abandon us. God intends to bless us and make us a blessing to others.

I thought of that as I went for a walk with a friend one morning. I counted my blessings: the fresh air and sunshine, the pink cherry trees already in bloom, a time that worked well for both of us, good health, and good conversation. She blessed me with words of encouragement, and I tried to do the same for her too. We talked about our new worship ministry for children, how we might meet the needs of young parents and bless the families of our church and neighborhood. Our "journey" was a simple walk around the neighborhood, but like Abram's journey, it, too, was a journey of blessing.

What challenges do you face in your journey with God at this point in your life? In what ways do you experience God's blessing, and how can you share that with others?

FAMILY RESEMBLANCE
ROMANS 4:1-5, 13-17

"You laugh just like Popo," says my niece, referring to her grandmother who is my mother.

"You and your sisters are so close even though you live at a distance," observes a friend. "You're always e-mailing each other."

"I thought you were her daughter," said one of the nurses when I went to see my mother-in-law in the hospital. "You look so much like her."

What identifies any group of people as family? It might be a shared characteristic like the way I laugh like my mother, or stir an egg into fried rice like my father. It might be the childhood and youthful memories that I share with my three sisters, sustained by an ongoing interest in on another's lives and almost daily communication. Family members might be bound together by shared joys and inside jokes that no one else understands, and by hugs and caring presence during times of crisis. At other times, family connection may mean a physical resemblance, like a similar height, short hair, oval-shaped eye-glasses, and high cheek-bones.

When it comes to the family of God, Romans 4 mentions several possible sources of unity and family resemblance. It begins with a reference to Abraham as an ancestor on "the basis of genealogy" (verse 1), or what the *New Revised Standard Version* calls "according to the flesh." In other words, we might think of family as bound together by biology and the sheer physicality of life. As a Jew and descendant of Abraham, the apostle Paul could claim that kind of connection with Abraham. So perhaps it's not surprising that he begins with the common ancestry that he shared with other Jewish Christians. They had a physical link passed from one generation to the next generation to the next, stretching from Abraham and Sarah all the way down through the centuries to Paul and the other Jewish members of the Roman church.

Their biological link was further reinforced in "the flesh" (NRSV) by various physical traditions, like the practice of circumcision, the practice of animal sacrifice, the way they kept the Sabbath, and many more practices related to temple worship and daily living. But, says Paul in our text, Abraham was not justified by these things, but by his faith.

The Gentile Christians of the Roman church could not claim the same physical link to Abraham—they did not share the same physical DNA or the same physical practices—but Abraham was still their ancestor according to faith. Abraham believed God, and so did they. God counted Abraham's faith as righteousness, not because of anything that Abraham had done, but as a gift of God's mercy on the basis of Abraham's faith. So too, God had mercy on both Gentile and Jewish Christians through Jesus Christ as a gift. It was not biology and the physicality of life that bound the church in Rome together, but faith. By faith, both Jewish and Gentile Christians could claim Abraham as their ancestor.

In verses 13-15 of our text, Paul goes on to demonstrate the inadequacy of the Law as a possible marker of the family of God. The Law had played a significant role in shaping the Israelite people who had been delivered from their slavery in Egypt to form a new community of God's people. The Law had become an integral part of their identity. But just as God's promise could not be attained by human ancestry, so too the Law could not accomplish God's promise (Romans 4:14). The role of the Law had been to point out sin—to highlight "violation" as in verse 15—and to place some boundaries around it. But the Law could not provide a remedy for sin. To inherit God's promise, those who followed the Law needed faith just as much as those who were outside the Law. Again, for both Jewish and Gentile Christians, faith became the deciding factor. God's promise depended on God's grace, not on human ancestry or on the Law.

For the church as the people of God today, our defining mark, our true family resemblance, also resides in our faith. In my congregation, we have several three-generation families with grandparents, parents, and grandchildren all sharing in the life of the church. What a wonderful blessing both to the members of those families and to all of us as a congregation! But those beautiful family relationships are not what makes us a church. Others who are not related by birth, adoption, or marriage are just as much a part of the church, for what binds us together is our shared faith in God and our shared walk with Jesus in the power of the Holy Spirit. As one new member shared in her testimony, "I'm not here because I'm related to anyone else in the church. I'm here because of Jesus." That's true for all of us: for the church of Rome who received this letter first and for all of us who claim Christ's name today.

The same holds true when it comes to the Law. At one time, in my community, stores were closed on Sundays. That meant no grocery shopping, no shopping for school supplies for the next day, no hanging out at the mall on Sunday afternoons. Local schools wouldn't even plan sporting events on Wednesdays because that was church youth night. Those customs or "laws" weren't on the same level as the Mosaic Law for the Jewish people, but they still helped to form a sense of community, a shared way of life, that some still mourn now that Sunday shopping and soccer and other sports on Wednesdays have become commonplace.

While those shared customs helped shape the life of my community, they weren't meant to accomplish God's promises any more than the Ten Commandments or the rest of the Mosaic law were meant to accomplish them. For people newly released from slavery, the Mosaic law offered a vision for living in healthy community together, but it did not have the power to transform or empower them. In this, God's grace surpasses the Law. For them, for the Roman church, and for us today, God's grace comes to us not by birth or Law, but by faith.

So what identifies people as part of the family of God? The good news is that you don't have to be born into a particular ethnic group or into the "right" family. You can't earn a place by doing the right thing. Instead, says Romans 4, the defining characteristic is to have faith like Abraham's: a faith that believed God's promise, a faith that trusted God for the journey, a faith that acknowledged God as the Creator and Giver of Life.

For Abraham, God's promise was still in the future. For us, God's promise has already come in Jesus. How much more, then, may we continue to believe in God's promise. How much more may we trust God for our own journey through life; how much more may we acknowledge God as the Creator who sustains our lives. That's our family resemblance as part of the family of faith.

What role do shared practices and shared traditions play in forming your congregation as a unified body? How has faith transformed your life—at home, in the church, and in your community and world?

COME TO JESUS
JOHN 3:1-17

Nicodemus

"Have you been born again?" called out the man on the street. He wore a long, ragged coat and carried a handful of pamphlets. Most people seemed to ignore him as they hurried by, and I thought seriously about crossing the street before I got to the corner where he stood. Instead, I buried my hands further into my pockets, and when he tried to give me a pamphlet, I shook my head. "Have you been born again?" he demanded.

"Yes, I have been," I said.

"Saved by the blood of Jesus?"

"Yes."

"Then praise the Lord!"

"Praise the Lord," I called back as I kept walking.

Although I answered yes to the man's question, I don't really know what he meant by being "born again," and I wondered what the other passersby thought that day. Were they also tempted to cross the street as I was? Did they hear being "born again" as a kind of code for a certain brand of fundamentalism? Did they know that Jesus first uses the phrase in conversation with a Jewish leader named Nicodemus? Only instead of a busy street corner, their encounter takes place alone at night, and it's Nicodemus who first approaches Jesus.

Nicodemus greets Jesus with a compliment, addressing him with respect as "rabbi," acknowledging him as a teacher, mentioning the miraculous signs that he has done, and recognizing God's presence with him (John 3:2). Some might speculate that Nicodemus comes to Jesus at night out of fear for what other people might think. Or perhaps his reason is less politically charged and more practical, to seek out Jesus for a private conversation without the crowds that usually gathered around him during the day. For whatever reason, Nicodemus makes his way to Jesus one night, and their conversation quickly focuses on being born again into God's kingdom. Nicodemus struggles to understand the meaning of Jesus' words in verse 3: "I assure you, unless someone is born anew, it's not possible to see God's kingdom."

The expression that Jesus uses here for being born "anew" can have at least three different meanings. It could well mean being born "again" in the sense of being born a second time, which is how Nicodemus understands it quite literally at first. He seems to assume that Jesus means a second, physical birth, for he asks, "How is it possible for an adult to be born?" (verse 4). That would be physically impossible!

Jesus then makes it clear that the second birth he has in mind is not physical, but spiritual, for he clarifies that "unless someone is born of water and the Spirit, it's not possible to enter God's kingdom" (verse 5, emphasis added). His clarification fits well with a second meaning of being born "anew" in the sense of being born "from above." This is not a physical birth, but metaphorical language to describe a spiritual birth—what might be called a heavenly birth, accomplished by God, not something that we can do ourselves.

A third meaning is to understand being born "anew" as being born "from the beginning"—to go back in time to the roots, before any other growth has begun, and to be reborn from the beginning. It means a thoroughgoing rebirth, a radical change to a completely new kind of life. This is the "eternal life" of verse 16; Jesus speaks not simply of life that goes on and on without end, but of life in the kingdom of God which means a new quality of life where there is joy and peace in the presence of God. That life is radically different, reborn from the beginning.

These three meanings come together in our text. For Jesus, being born again means to have a second, spiritual birth accomplished by God that changes us completely and ushers in a radically new kind of life. It's a rebirth into God's kingdom. Like Nicodemus, we might want to ask, "How are these things possible?" (verse 9). How can we be born anew? Does this second, spiritual birth depend on our physical birth into the "right" family? No. Do we need to be educated and a community leader like Nicodemus? No. Do we need to follow a certain set of laws? No. Do we need to say a prayer with just the right words asking Jesus into our hearts and lives? No. In our text, the key to eternal life is simply to believe in Jesus. That was Jesus' challenge to Nicodemus, and it's God's challenge for us today (verses 10-16).

Nicodemus leaves behind no formal statement of faith, no personal testimony expressing his belief, no declaration that he has indeed been born anew. Instead, the Gospel of John shows some of his belief in action. In our text, Nicodemus clearly believes enough to seek out Jesus. Later, when the chief priests and Pharisees try to convince the guards to arrest Jesus, Nicodemus believes enough to speak up against them: "Our Law doesn't judge someone without first hearing him and learning what he is doing, does it?" (John 7:51). After Jesus' death, when Joseph of Arimathea asks for his body, Nicodemus believes enough to go with him, and together they bury Jesus, wrapping his body in linen cloths with nearly seventy-five pounds of spices that Nicodemus had brought with him—myrrh and aloe according to their traditional burial customs (John 19:38-42).

From these few snapshots in John's Gospel, Nicodemus appears to be a sincere and thoughtful seeker; a man who asks good questions and stands for what is right even in the face of criticism by others; a man who expresses courage, compassion, and generosity after Jesus' death. "But was he born again?" as the man on the street corner might want to ask. Perhaps that's a question best left for heaven, for our text doesn't answer it directly. While the behavior of Nicodemus seems persuasive, he leaves behind no conclusive proof one way or the other. Instead, his story seems to be open-ended, as if to leave us wondering both about Nicodemus and about our own unfinished stories.

Each time Nicodemus appears in John's Gospel, he is identified as the one who had come to Jesus (3:2; 7:50; 19:39). That seems to be the best starting place for us today too. Whether we think of ourselves as "born again" or not, come to Jesus. Whether we are new to faith or long-time believers, come to Jesus. Whether we welcome the idea of testimony or shy away from it, come to Jesus. Come with questions; come with doubts; come with however much or little you have to offer. Just come to Jesus.

In what ways have you been born anew? In what ways are you still living in the past, holding on to old grudges, repeating old habits, hanging back from the radically new life that God offers?

Psalm 121

[1] I raise my eyes toward the mountains.
  Where will my help come from?
[2] My help comes from the LORD,
  the maker of heaven and earth.
[3] God won't let your foot slip.
  Your protector won't fall asleep on the job.
[4] No! Israel's protector
  never sleeps or rests!
[5] The LORD is your protector;
  the LORD is your shade right beside you.
[6] The sun won't strike you during the day;
  neither will the moon at night.
[7] The LORD will protect you from all evil;
  God will protect your very life.
[8] The LORD will protect you on your journeys—
  whether going or coming—
  from now until forever from now.

GROUP STUDY GUIDE

Questions for Discussion

1. In Romans 4, Paul says that workers are paid what their work deserves, but those who receive God's grace don't have to work for it. All they need is faith (verses 4-5). Yet even Abram apparently put his faith to work by setting out on his journey. The Letter of James flatly declares, "faith without actions is dead" (James 2:26). How, then, are work and faith related in Christian living? What does this mean personally for you?

2. "Born again," "eternal life," and other Christian terms can sometimes seem like specialized language for insiders. How would you rephrase John 3:16 to communicate well with a neighbor or coworker unfamiliar with Christian jargon?

3. Compare and contrast Abram and Nicodemus. Consider God's work in their lives and how each responded, their faith, and the risks they each faced. What can you learn from their experiences?

4. Some athletes and other celebrities use their public platform to give verbal witness to their Christian faith. Where have you seen that done well, in ways that express genuine faith as well as respect for others? In what ways has it seemed disrespectful or otherwise inappropriate?

5. How do you share your faith with others in your family, neighborhood, and wider community and world? Do you tend to emphasize words, actions, or both equally?

Suggestions for Group Study

Prayer Walk

Take a prayer walk around your neighborhood. Before you leave, read Psalm 121, a psalm meant to be read by pilgrims on their way to the temple in Jerusalem. As they looked forward to their destination, the psalm reminded them of God's help and protection along the way. As you walk, what do you notice along your way? Offer a prayer of thanks for the blessings that you see. Ask God's help for the needs that surround you.

Consider Your Feelings

Close your eyes and imagine yourself on the street walking toward the man with the long, ragged coat and fistful of pamphlets described in the reflection above. "Have you been born again?" he calls out. How do you feel about this encounter? Sit with your feelings for a moment before exploring them further with the group. Next, imagine you are Nicodemus, a teacher and leader among your people, hoping for a quiet conversation with Jesus. How do you feel when he says, "You must be born anew" (John 3:7)? Sit with those feelings for a moment before exploring them further with the group. How are your feelings the same or different from your feelings in the first scenario?

Closing Prayer

O God who calls us, journeys with us, and goes before us, we long to walk with you. Grant us courage to step out in faith. Calm our fears, and teach us to rely on you for the risks that lie ahead. Make us good traveling companions who encourage, strengthen, and comfort one another. For the journey of each day, for the longer arc of our journey through life, open our eyes to your goodness. As we have received your blessing, be our help as we bless those around us. Be our hope for the future. Amen.

Renewed by the Spirit

Scriptures for the
Third Sunday of Lent
Exodus 17:1-7
Romans 5:1-11
John 4:5-42

"Water, water, everywhere, Nor any drop to drink," wrote Samuel Taylor Coleridge in *The Rime of the Ancient Mariner*. Adrift on the silent sea day after day, the ancient mariner and his crew became more and more thirsty—so parched they could not speak, although surrounded by water on all sides as far as they could see.

With water covering over seventy percent of the earth's surface, we might also think of ourselves as surrounded by water. And Coleridge's poetic lines still hold true for millions of people around the world who lack access to clean drinking water. Water, water, over most of the earth, while many still look for a clean drop to drink. What's more, according to the United Nations, every continent is touched by some form of water scarcity, whether from uneven distribution, waste, pollution, or other factors (See *www.un.org/waterforlifedecade/scarcity.shtml*). Yet water remains essential for life—for human beings, for other creatures, and for the entire ecosystem.

How fitting, then, that in Scripture water often appears as a metaphor for spiritual renewal. In Psalm 42:1-2, the psalmist says, "Just like a deer that craves streams of water, my whole being craves you, God. My whole being thirsts for God, for the living God." In Revelation 21:6, this spiritual thirst finds satisfaction from the One seated on the throne: "All is done. I am the Alpha and the Omega, the beginning and the end. To the thirsty I will freely give water from the life-giving spring." Just as our bodies need physical water to sustain life and to function well, so we also need the water of spiritual renewal to flourish as whole human beings.

All four of the lectionary texts for this week allude to water as a word picture for spiritual renewal. In John 4, when Jesus speaks with a woman at the well, he asks for a drink of water because he is tired and thirsty. Then he offers her living water because he senses that she is thirsty too—thirsty for a renewed life of the Spirit that only he could give. For the Israelite people in the wilderness, their physical thirst for water has a spiritual dimension as Moses takes their complaint to God (Exodus 17:1-17), and as the psalmist later remembers their experience and turns it into a psalm of praise (Psalm 95). Even in Romans 5:1-11, while the text doesn't mention water directly, the water of spiritual renewal appears there too in God's love "*poured out* in our hearts through the Holy Spirit" (verse 5, emphasis added).

So this Lenten season, come, if you're thirsty. Come, even if you're not. Just as drinking water before you feel thirsty is the best way to avoid dehydration, so the spiritual water of life can begin to renew us even before we become spiritually drained and dry. May God's living water spring up before us and in us, that we might flourish and share living water with those around us.

REST AND RELEASE
EXODUS 17:1-7

As the Israelite people made their way from Egypt toward the Promised Land, they stopped to camp at Rephidim. This place name is related to a Hebrew verb meaning "refresh" or "support," so we might take this to mean that they stopped at a place called "refreshment" or "resting places." But instead of resting in God's care and provision, the people complained that they had no water to drink and began to argue with Moses. Just as they had complained about the bitter water at Marah (Exodus 15:22-25), and just as Moses had called on God's help at that time, here too, the people complained to Moses and Moses turned to God.

Once again, God met the people in their time of need in a miraculous way. In that dry desert, the Lord directed Moses and a few of the elders to a rock at Horeb, and when Moses struck the rock with his staff, the people received fresh water. From that time, the place became known as Massah (which means test) and Meribah (which means argument), because the people had tested and argued with the Lord.

I wonder why Moses chose to memorialize the people's complaint in the place names instead of highlighting God's miraculous provision. I think I'd be more inclined to call the place Fresh-Water-From-the-Rock, or God-Gave-Us-Water, or The-Lord-Answers-Prayer. Wouldn't a more positive name serve just as well as a reminder to the people? Why then key in on their testing and arguing?

Perhaps that emphasis captured more fully the intensity of the experience for Moses. After all, the people not only complained against the Lord; more personally and pointedly, they argued against Moses himself. "Why did *you* bring us out of Egypt to kill us?" they demanded (verse 3, emphasis added). They were so angry that Moses feared for his life. "What should I do with this people?" he cried out to God. "They are getting ready to stone me" (verse 4). While the water flowing from the rock satisfied the people's thirst, it also saved Moses' life.

In a reference to this story, the psalmist tells his readers, "Don't harden your hearts like you did at Meribah, like you did when you were at Massah, in the wilderness, when your ancestors tested me and scrutinized me, even though they had already seen my acts" (Psalm 95:8-9). In this context, the place names serve as warnings: Don't test God. Don't argue against God. Remember how the people complained, and God acted in a powerful way. The same God at work in the past is the same God at work today.

We need that reminder too, for it's all too easy to slip into complaint mode. The weather's too hot, or too cold, or too wet. The hot water tank broke down, so the laundry has to wait. I'm stuck in traffic and late for my appointment. My coworker always seems to have an excuse to leave early and leave me with extra work. My parents/kids/grandkids/siblings don't understand me. The music at church is too loud. The singing is too slow. Why are the same people always the ones to volunteer? Where are all the young people? Why doesn't God just do something??

Some of our complaints may hold a core of truth that can spur us to personal action. It's time to install a new hot water tank. Tomorrow, I won't try to cram so much into my morning and will leave earlier. I need to talk with my coworker about how we balance our workload.

How can we be more creative in engaging people of all ages in worship and the work of the church? Can we try something new?

Some of our complaints may express legitimate community and social concerns. Clean water remains a critical need in our time. Refugees and other displaced people still need shelter and a place to call home. Domestic and sexual abuse, hunger and poverty, racism and other forms of oppression, violence and war . . . we need to bring these situations to God and cry out! Not simply to complain, but to pray earnestly for God's power at work, for the Spirit to descend and heal our brokenness, for Jesus to walk with us as we seek to listen, to be present with those who suffer, and to work toward constructive response.

But sometimes when we complain, we're simply whining and need to be brought up short. At least, I do anyway. Stop complaining, says Massah. Stop whining, says Meribah. Set aside your first-world problems, and be thankful. The laundry can wait. Let the music be a joyful noise to the Lord. It's okay if the people in your life don't understand you perfectly. Remember how God has provided for you in the past, and trust God for your present and future. Don't test God. Don't argue. Trust.

A few years ago, instead of a New Year's resolution, I chose just one key word to help give focus to my year. My one word was "release," a word that came to me in the midst of preparing for Christmas. I still needed to write my annual Christmas letter, send out cards, buy a few more gifts to mail away, find readers for Christmas Eve, plan the Christmas Day service, figure out what I was going to bring to the Christmas Day potluck, get ready for our family Christmas on the following day. . . . Whew! It seemed as if my to-do list was getting longer instead of shorter.

"But why? Why take on all of those things?" said the still, small voice underneath all of my hectic preparations. Why not simply release them? I imagined myself releasing my life to God—not only for the Christmas season, but for the coming year—letting go of the things I clutched so tightly and allowing more room for God's Spirit to work.

I started practicing that Christmas, and *release* became my word for the new year, a word that I kept coming back to again and again. Instead of complaining that I had too much to do, I let some things go, not because they were bad but because they were simply too much. Some things were taken up by others; some things simply faded away.

As I practiced releasing again and again, I discovered again and again that God remained faithful and granted me renewal.

When the year was over, I moved on to a new word, but living with "release" for that year was a healthy and helpful discipline for me. I think it would have helped the Israelite people too. Instead of longing for Egypt and remembering it as so much better than it was, what if they had been able to release their old life of slavery and embrace God's new future for them? What if they had rested in the faithfulness and sure provision of God instead of complaining at Massah and Meribah? Perhaps then Rephidim might have truly been their resting place.

How much of your complaining has resulted in positive action and prayer, and how much has simply been whining? What is your favorite way to find release and rest from complaining?

HOLY BOASTING
ROMANS 5:1-11

In the history of the Christian church, pride takes its place as one of the seven deadly sins—"deadly" because it can destroy the life of the Spirit in us, along with its partners of greed, lust, envy, gluttony, wrath, and sloth. "Pride comes before disaster, and arrogance before a fall," says Proverbs 16:18. Instead of pride, 1 Peter 5:5-6 urges readers, "clothe yourselves with humility toward each other. God stands against the proud, but he gives favor to the humble. Therefore, humble yourselves under God's power so that he may raise you up in the last day." Even Christ Jesus—as Lord of all before the creation of the world—"humbled" himself to become human and die a horrible death (Philippians 2:8).

Yet Paul speaks positively about pride in Romans 5:1-11. "We even take pride in God," says the closing verse, capping off the previous verses that describe God's work in Jesus Christ. God loved us long before we realized it, and sent Jesus to live, die, and rise again to restore our relationship with God. We can take pride that God did all of that without our having to work for it or to prove ourselves worthy. Because of the hope we have in God's glory, we can boast! says verse 2. We can even take pride in our problems, says verse 3.

So on the one hand, there's the kind of pride that goes before a fall, that has no place in Christian community, that perhaps even led to Satan's disgrace as a fallen angel (as Isaiah 14:12-15 has been traditionally interpreted). On the other hand, these verses from Romans encourage pride as the best response in light of all that God has done for us. Paul speaks not just of a quiet, beaming pride in a job well done, but of a delightful boasting. What's the difference then between pride as deadly sin and pride as this holy, exuberant celebration?

In the Letter to the Romans, the Greek word for pride or bragging appears only in these verses. But in a letter to the church of Corinth, Paul uses the noun form of the word to chastise his readers for their approval of sexual immorality in the church. "Your bragging isn't good," he admonishes them (1 Corinthians 5:6). The Letter of James applies the same word to the rich who focus on their own plans with no concern for God's will in their lives: "But now you boast and brag, and all such boasting is evil" (James 4:16). On both of these occasions, the boasting came from those who chose to go their own way instead of setting their sights on God's way, and their boast centered on their own misguided judgment.

In contrast, in our Romans text, boasting is centered on God who showed us such great love in Jesus, who has made us righteous and saved us by the death of Christ, who has reconciled us to God. The text begins and ends with peace and reconciliation: "We have peace with God" (verse 1), and "we have been reconciled" (verse 10). But we can't take any of the credit. All of the glory belongs to God, who sent Jesus, and so changed human history and changed our lives. We can boast in the work of God through Jesus Christ.

We can even be proud of our problems, not because of the problems themselves or because we can solve them on our own, but because God can transform even our problems. That might not be readily apparent when we're in the midst of our difficulties, but by the grace of God, we're not left to struggle alone. As the Spirit of God continues its transforming work in our lives, our troubles can lead to endurance, character, and hope. We can boast in the work of God in our own lives as God transforms us.

So then, the difference between a deadly pride and a holy pride depends on the object of our boasting. If our intention is simply to boast in ourselves and in our own accomplishments, then watch out! That's the kind of pride that goes before a fall, for it ignores our dependence on God and also fails to recognize how much we owe to others. But if we boast in the Lord, we place the emphasis where it belongs: on God who is the source of our being, the lover of our souls, our all in all.

One way we can boast in the Lord is in our worship. The word *worship* comes from an Old English word that means "worth-ship;" so in worship, we proclaim God's worth. In other words, we take pride in all that God is and does. We boast about God's supreme value. Hymns like "Holy, Holy, Holy! Lord God Almighty" and "Immortal, Invisible, God Only Wise" boast in God's power, purity, love, mercy, creativity, grace, and glory. "Amazing Grace" boasts in God's saving and transforming power that carries us through our troubles and leads us home at last. "10,000 Reasons (Bless the Lord)" proudly proclaims God's love, kindness, patience, and goodness.

Besides the songs we sing and listen to, the spoken parts of our worship also provide opportunity for the kind of holy boasting described in our Romans text. In our prayers for the needs of our church and world, we call upon God who is almighty and gracious; Our Father who is in heaven; the great Creator, Redeemer, and Sustainer; and other names that take pride in who God is and how God relates to us. In litanies, testimonies, Scripture readings, and sermons we tell of God's saving work in history and how God remains at work around the world and in our personal, household, and church life today. In worship, we're boasting!

When we focus on God with that kind of praise-filled pride, there's no room for the pride that focuses on ourselves and our own accomplishments. We sing God's praises instead of our own. We testify to God's work in our lives. In our prayers, we acknowledge our dependence on God. Worship thus reorients us to boast in the Lord instead of boasting in ourselves.

In what ways do you feel proud of God? How does your understanding and practice of worship change when you think about it as boasting about the Lord?

LIVING WATER
JOHN 4:5-42

Jesus had every reason to ignore the woman at the well. In the world of John's Gospel, it was highly inappropriate for Jesus to initiate a public conversation with this woman. Especially since he was regarded as a rabbi. Especially since she had been married five times and wasn't even married to her current partner. Especially since Jews and Samaritans had nothing to do with one another, as our Gospel text points out (verse 9).

The two groups both traced their roots back to Abraham, but the Samaritans hailed from the old northern kingdom of Israel, and the Jews from the old southern kingdom of Judah. The Jews worshiped in the temple in Jerusalem, while the Samaritans had their own sacred site on Mount Gerizim. In the time of Jesus, the two groups were so estranged that many Jews would not even travel through the land of Samaria. To go from Judea in the south to Galilee in the north, they would detour around Samaria even though that made for a much longer trip.

In the preamble to our text, John 4:4 says that "Jesus *had to go* through Samaria" (emphasis added). Humanly speaking that just wasn't so, since Jesus could have made the same detour around Samaria like so many other Jews. But Jesus had a larger purpose in mind, for by traveling through Samaria he demonstrated that what he had to offer was not only for the Jews, but for the Samaritans too, and indeed, for the whole world. In John's Gospel, Jesus traveled from Jerusalem (John 2:23) to Judea (John 3:22) to Samaria (John 4:4) just as he would later tell his disciples "you will be my witnesses in Jerusalem, in all Judea and Samaria, and to the end of the earth" (Acts 1:8). His own movements set the stage. So Jesus deliberately traveled through Samaria, stopped to rest at the Samaritan town of Sychar, and spoke to the woman at the well.

In asking her for a drink of water, Jesus reached across the religious, social, cultural, and moral barriers that separated them. He initiated a cross-cultural conversation, a male-female conversation, and an interfaith conversation all at once, and all by asking for a drink of water. For her part, the woman responded with curiosity, with good questions, with a level of engagement that ultimately transformed her life and the lives of those around her.

Their conversation began on common ground—not with their obvious differences, but with their common need for water. Jesus was thirsty, and the woman had a water jar. The woman turned out to be thirsty too, and Jesus had living water to offer her. Both had something to share. Both had something to receive.

While Jesus found common ground with the woman in their common need for water, he wasn't afraid to acknowledge their differences. While he respected her views and her questions, he also gave clear witness to his own identity. He offered her living water, not just a taste or a cupful, but a never-ending spring of water bubbling up to eternal life (John 4:14). Just as Romans 5:5 speaks of God's love so generously "poured out," so the living water of John 4:14 is so generously given that whoever drinks of it will never be thirsty again. The living water meant spiritual renewal, a new relationship with God that would change the Samaritan woman at the well, change the people of her city, and can change us today.

For the woman at the well, renewal meant admitting the reality of her life including her previous five husbands and her current partner. Renewal meant discovering a new way to worship in Spirit and in truth. Renewal meant this encounter with Jesus that was so unexpected and so genuine that she left her water jar at the well, and hurried back to the city to tell everyone she knew about Jesus. Whether she had the words to explain it or not, she had that spring of water bubbling up and spilling over to share with everyone she knew. Even though she still had questions—"Could this man be the Christ?" (John 4:29)—she was still eager to share her experience and to extend Jesus' invitation to others. Then because of the woman's testimony and because of Jesus' own word, many of the Samaritans of her city found spiritual renewal too; they believed and came to know Jesus as the Savior of the world. Could it be?

Last year, I spoke at a denominational leadership day on the theme of spiritual renewal for changing times. In the face of great changes in our culture and in the church, much attention has centered on how best to respond to the changes around us. But for that day, I was asked to shift the focus. I was to concentrate not so much on what to do or what not to do *about* change, or how to adjust to change or hold our ground, but on how to find spiritual renewal *in the midst* of changing times. How can we find spiritual renewal for ourselves personally, for our congregations, and for our communities?

What a delight to spend an entire day with pastors, chaplains, and other church leaders, all focused on spiritual renewal. Each of my three sessions included a Scripture focus, some teaching, and a spiritual exercise or group discussion. We read Scripture, worshiped in song, practiced *lectio divina*, prayed together, shared stories, reflected in silence, laughed, ate, discussed, questioned. It was a full day, and yet even as the speaker, I felt renewed by our time together.

As I reflect back on that day, however, I realize that the renewal didn't really come from the stories or silence or laughing together. It didn't come from what I had shared with the group, although my talks had been the product of long hours and bathed in prayer. No, those things were only the avenues of spiritual renewal that God used that day, and through them, we encountered Jesus. By his Spirit present with us, he was our source of living water, just as he had been for the woman at the well.

It's a long way from the Samaritan city of Sychar to the life we live today. In North America, people of different religious and cultural backgrounds live and work together in the same cities with fewer restrictions than Jesus and the Samaritan woman experienced. Men more freely talk with women in public settings. Divorce, remarriage, and living together have become commonplace. But people still get thirsty for spiritual renewal, and spiritual renewal still comes through meeting Jesus.

What barriers to spiritual renewal can you identify in our world today? What spiritual practices, attitudes, or other avenues of spiritual renewal help you to meet Jesus?

1 Come, let's sing out loud to the LORD!
   Let's raise a joyful shout to the rock of our salvation!
2 Let's come before him with thanks!
   Let's shout songs of joy to him!
3 The LORD is a great God,
   the great king over all other gods.
4 The earth's depths are in his hands;
   the mountain heights belong to him;
5   the sea, which he made, is his
      along with the dry ground,
      which his own hands formed.
6 Come, let's worship and bow down!
   Let's kneel before the LORD, our maker!
7 He is our God,
   and we are the people of his pasture,
   the sheep in his hands.
If only you would listen to his voice right now!
8   "Don't harden your hearts
   like you did at Meribah,
   like you did when you were at Massah,
      in the wilderness,
9   when your ancestors tested me
      and scrutinized me,
   even though they had already seen my acts.
10 For forty years I despised that generation;
   I said, 'These people have twisted hearts.
   They don't know my ways.'
11 So in anger I swore:
   'They will never enter my place of rest!' "

GROUP STUDY GUIDE

Questions for Discussion

1. Water makes a powerful metaphor for spiritual renewal. But just as our bodies may actually need water before we feel physically thirsty, our spirits may also need renewal before we feel spiritually thirsty. How can we become more aware of our need for God? Is it possible to cultivate spiritual thirst?

2. When the people of Israel first entered the desert, they had good reason to complain, for they traveled for three days without finding water until God miraculously provided for them (Exodus 15:22-25). By Exodus 17:1-7, however, they apparently hadn't yet learned to trust God fully, for they again complain, and God miraculously provides. What spiritual lessons are you still learning? What places of Massah and Meribah can you identify in your life—places or times when you have struggled and wondered whether God was with you?

3. Romans 5:1-11 begins and ends with peace and reconciliation— "peace with God" (verse 1) and "reconciled to God" (verse 10). According to this text, how are peace and reconciliation with God accomplished? What difference does this peace make in how we understand sin and deal with the challenges of daily living?

4. In John 4, most of the action takes place between Jesus and the woman at the well while Jesus' disciples are in the city buying food. Notice what happens when the disciples return (verses 27-38). How do you think the woman would have answered their unspoken question: "What do you want?" How would Jesus have answered, "Why are you talking with her"?

5. The theme of God's provision runs through the lectionary texts for this week. In Exodus, God provided water for the Israelites in the desert, which is noted also in Psalm 95. In the Gospel of John, God provided living water for the Samaritan woman and her people. In Romans, God gives us peace, confidence, and hope through Jesus Christ. As you reflect on your personal history, how has God provided for you physically and spiritually?

Suggestions for Group Study

Explore World Water Day

Do some Internet research on the United Nations World Water Day, which is March 22. Begin at the following website to learn about water use and challenges around the world: *www.unwater.org/worldwaterday*. Browse through the suggested activities and consider choosing one as a group. Or share your own ideas for using less water or caring for the waterways in your area. Commit to one of these ideas throughout the rest of Lent. Discuss how caring for and preserving water might be a faithful Christian witness to Jesus as the one who provides "living water."

Make a Toast

Pour a glass of water for everyone in your group, and then take turns offering toasts of praise to God. What makes you proud of who God is, or what God has done for you? As with any good toast, be brief, genuine, and personal. Read Psalm 95:1-7 as a proclamation of God's greatness. Then sing one of the songs mentioned in this chapter that give worth to God, or choose one or more songs of your own. Think of this as a time of worship and boasting in the Lord.

Closing Prayer

From the magnitude of world problems and pressing needs, we come to you, O God, seeking relief and renewal. From the weariness and trials of daily living, we come to you, O God, seeking a better way. Be our rest to comfort our fears and grant us peace. Be our living water that refreshes us daily and satisfies our thirst. Be our pride and source of joy for you provide us with every good thing. Amen.

A Study in Contrasts

Scriptures for the
Fourth Sunday of Lent
1 Samuel 16:1-13
Ephesians 5:8-14
John 9:1-41

In art, the contrast of light and dark areas of a painting has been called *chiaroscuro,* an Italian word literally meaning light-dark. The strong contrasts of light and dark may be used to add contour or volume to a human figure. Or they can add drama to a scene, as if it's lit by a single shaft of light. In some paintings of the Nativity, the infant Jesus radiates a divine light that bathes and adds contours to the entire composition. While chiaroscuro may be most well known with reference to painting, it may also describe the contrast of light and dark in photography and cinematography as well.

We might think of this week's texts as another kind of chiaroscuro, for they, too, present a strong contrast between light and dark, which is reinforced by the related themes of sight and blindness. We see this most clearly in the Ephesians text, which contrasts the readers' former darkness with their new status as children of light. The fruit of the light contrasts with the unfruitful works of darkness. What is visible contrasts with what is shameful. The text then ends with a call to the one sleeping in the dark to wake up into the shining light of Christ.

For both 1 Samuel 16 and John 9, the theme of sight is prominent. In the Old Testament text, the contrast lies between God's sight on the inside and human sight on the outside. Even as the text emphasizes how God looks on the heart in choosing Jesse's youngest son, the oh-so-human narrator still looks on the outside and can't resist commenting on how handsome David is. In the New Testament text, the man who was born blind—who has lived in "darkness" all of his life—receives both physical and spiritual sight, and so comes into the light.

In this week's Psalm, we might imagine the psalmist walking in sunshine through grassy meadows, beside still waters, and finally through "the darkest valley," or what the King James Version calls "the valley of the shadow of death" (Psalm 23:4). Yet in every circumstance, in the full light of day and the darkest night, the psalmist relies on the presence of the Good Shepherd. As Fanny Crosby wrote in her popular gospel song, "All the way my Savior leads me, What have I to ask beside? Can I doubt His tender mercy, Who through life has been my Guide?"

For us too, life may seem a study in contrasts between light and dark, good times and trial, celebration and mourning, health and sickness, hurt and healing. And through it all we have the Savior as our guide, the One who shepherds us through light and dark, dark and light, whatever the future may hold. Christ is for us, to shine a light in our darkness, and even more, to *be* the light that the darkness can never extinguish.

HOW IS YOUR HEART?
1 SAMUEL 16:1-13

Samuel had a problem. In response to God's word, he had anointed Saul as king over Israel (1 Samuel 10:1), and now the word of the Lord had come to him again to anoint a new king from among the sons of Jesse of Bethlehem. How could this be? God had rejected Saul as king because of his disobedience (1 Samuel 15), but practically speaking Saul still reigned as king. To anoint someone in his place amounted to treason, which was punishable by death. Yet in spite of Samuel's misgivings, the Lord directed him to anoint the one who would be shown to him. What was Samuel to do?

The elders of Bethlehem had a problem. They handled any disputes that arose among the people, and as long as things could be resolved, they managed to avoid any undue attention or interference by officials from beyond the city. That was by far the best for them as elders and for everyone in the community. But now Samuel had arrived, and his well-known status as a judge (1 Samuel 7:15-17) made them fearful. What did Samuel want, and what were the elders to do?

Jesse had a problem. He, too, shared the elders' view that it was best not to attract too much attention from any authority. He and his sons worked hard in the fields taking care of their livestock. Now Samuel was inviting him and his sons to join him in making a sacrifice to the Lord. There must be something more going on, but how was Jesse to know unless he agreed? Besides, given Samuel's stature as a judge, his invitation seemed less like a request and more like a command performance. What was Jesse to do?

As you consider this text, with whom do you most identify? Are you most like Samuel, faced with God's call, sensing the right thing to do in a particular situation, yet fearful to follow through? Are you most like the elders of the city, trying to do your best within your own circle of influence—your own family, your own work, your own church—and wary of any intrusions from the world beyond what you know? Are you most like Jesse, curious about a new opportunity and willing to explore? What are you to do about the challenges you face on a daily basis? You may not be a judge, or an elder, or a father, but you also face situations that require prayer, discernment, wisdom, and courage.

One of the key principles in this text is that "God doesn't look at things like humans do. Humans see only what is visible to the eyes, but the Lord sees into the heart" (verse 7). This certainly played out in the choice of the new king as Samuel considered and passed over Eliab, Abinadab, Shammah, and every other son that Jesse presented to him. They may have looked fine, but God was looking for something—for some *one*—else. "Is that all?" asked Samuel, and only then did Jesse call for his youngest son who had been outside taking care of the sheep. According to the narrator, David looked healthy and handsome, but God looked beyond his outward appearance to his heart, and that's what qualified him to be the new king.

That same contrast between outward appearance and invisible reality runs through the rest of the text. From the beginning of the chapter, outwardly Saul was still king with all of the honor and visible signs of royalty. That's why Samuel hesitated to anoint a new king in his place. But God showed Samuel a new reality not yet visible with David as king. Outwardly to the people of Bethlehem, Samuel had come to perform a sacrifice, but his real purpose not yet revealed was to anoint a new king. Even at the end of the text, while the Spirit of

God invisibly rested on David, outwardly David remained the youngest son of Jesse and returned to tending the sheep (1 Samuel 16:19).

What challenges, problems, or decisions do you face today, and how might the understanding in this text apply to your situation? Humanly speaking, what do you see on the outside? What are the benefits and drawbacks, the pros and cons of what you face? Then prayerfully consider, what might God see at the heart of the matter, and in the hearts of those involved? How is the Spirit at work? What might not be obvious to the outside observer, but will be revealed by the eyes of faith?

For the last few months, my heart has been heavy with my husband's abrupt loss of his teaching position due to the financial situation of the college where he has taught for twenty-six years. On top of that, our family has been struggling with the illness and death of my brother-in-law who was only in his mid-sixties. Outwardly, we've been grieving—shedding tears, making funeral arrangements, standing at the graveside, hugging our family and friends—but inwardly and invisibly, we are also being comforted and strengthened by the Spirit of God. We know that death is not the end—not the death of a job, nor the physical death of a loved one, nor the death of a dream. As human beings, we may look on the outside and react to the things that we see and experience. But God looks on the inside, to our hearts and to the invisible work of the Spirit.

With the eyes of faith, we too may catch a glimpse of the new reality that is just around the corner and not yet visible. I don't know all that it will look like, but I know that resurrection is coming one day for my brother-in-law and all who believe. Death is not the end. Resurrection means new life, and even now that new life is springing up around and within us. And yes, that means even during this season of Lent. Even in the face of death and deep loss.

I don't know all that resurrection means for the many adjustments that need to be made following the death of my brother-in-law. I don't know all that resurrection means for my husband's future employment. Job prospects seem bleak, as other Christian colleges like his are also struggling financially or even closing their doors. But however things might look on the outside, I know that this personal Lent of our lives will not last forever. We hold onto hope, for resurrection is coming. With the eyes of faith, even now we see Easter on the horizon.

What qualities do you think God was looking for in a new king? What did God see when he looked into David's heart? How is your heart today?

THE LIGHT REVEALS
EPHESIANS 5:8-14

Imagine a celebration of baptism or confirmation where this Ephesians text serves as the concluding words of joy and affirmation for the new members. "You were once darkness," they are told, "but now you are light in the Lord" (verse 8). Now they receive the challenge to live in that light, discerning what is pleasing and doing good. Their new life lies before them. After these words of encouragement, everyone who has gathered joins in a final song of blessing. The closing lines of our text offer a brief quote from that song, which calls out to someone asleep in the dark, urging the sleeper to wake up and come to the light of Christ.

As my small group considered this text, the words came alive as we imagined them in this setting of the church and baptism. They suddenly became less theoretical and more practical, less philosophical about the relationship between light and dark, and more embedded in the living of daily life. What does it mean to be children of light in our world today? Does that description fit us? What works of darkness should be exposed to the light so there can be positive change and healing? What is the place of confession in our personal, church, and public life?

The movie *Spotlight* tells the true story of how *Boston Globe* reporters shined a light on allegations of child sexual abuse and cover-up in the Catholic Church. Through their investigative journalism, what had remained hidden for decades finally came to light, and the revelations shook the religious and legal establishment in Boston and around the world. To use the language of Ephesians, what certain people did in secret became embarrassing in the light—not only embarrassing, but shown to be morally corrupt, criminal, and tragically destructive. The works of darkness were revealed. Those involved had clearly failed the "newspaper test" of ethical behavior: Don't do anything you wouldn't want to see reported in the newspaper headlines the next day.

More personally, how do we fare when it comes to living as children of light? Is the newspaper test an appropriate guide to help us navigate the ethical decisions that face us each day, or do we need something more or different? On the plus side, the newspaper test provides a quick, easily understood, and memorable standard for checking one's moral compass. But it's also clearly weighted toward self-interest, which focuses narrowly on personal ethics and fails to address the larger structural and institutional expressions of sin and evil in our world. Furthermore, while looking out for one's reputation may be one practical consideration, surely, sound Christian ethics must be guided by something more than self-regard. Our text points to a more comprehensive measure of Christian ethics grounded in "goodness, justice, and truth" (verse 9), which provide far more reliable guidance.

The sharp contrast in Ephesians between the former darkness and the present light might suggest an absolute opposition between the life of unbelief and the new life of faith, between the life of the world and the new life as part of God's kingdom as represented by the church. But life does not divide neatly into a strict dualism. There is much in "the world" that is beautiful, good, and life-giving, and too much in the church that remains flawed and unjust, even to the extent of sexual abuse and cover-up as *The Boston Globe* investigative team discovered.

If we are honest with ourselves, we know that mix of dark and light runs through our own hearts and lives too. As the apostle Paul lamented about himself, "I don't do the good that I want to do, but I do the evil that I don't want to do" (Romans 7:19). Anyone who has ever blurted out the wrong thing in anger, cut someone off in traffic, tried to get even, spread spiteful gossip, told a lie, walked by someone in need, refused to apologize for a wrong, stood by when someone else was being bullied, or committed any number of other sins by commission or omission, knows exactly what the apostle means. Even those of us who think we are doing well may be surprised. We may be children of light, but we reflect that light imperfectly in the life we live each day and by our participation in the structures of poverty, racism, and other systemic sin.

One of the men in my small group has a great way to describe it. He drives a school bus for a living, which means that he also carries the responsibility to wash all twenty-four windows on the bus. "But no matter how hard I try," he says, "no matter how clean I think I've gotten those windows, on a sunny day with the angle just right, I can still see all kinds of spots and streaks. The light reveals." In the same way, no matter how hard we try, our lives and our world may still have all kinds of spots and streaks when illuminated by the light of Christ. We all still stand in need of repentance and confession. We all still stand in need of God's grace.

As we repent, confess our failures, and receive God's forgiveness; we find freedom from the things that bind us and "reveal the truth about them" (verse 11). Sometimes, that confession takes place corporately in the context of worship; at other times as part of a smaller support group; at other times more personally as we confess to the one we have wronged and seek to be reconciled. When our confession is genuine, and by the grace of God at work in our lives, the works of darkness are exposed in the light, and we turn from them to live into the new life.

But what of the different forms of public confession that have become prevalent in our day? What of the official public apologies by governments, the tearful celebrities religious and otherwise, the websites where people can post their confessions anonymously? Some might dismiss these in turn as pure politics, or showy public relations, or sham confessions devoid of any personal responsibility or genuine accountability. "Are these really confessions?" we might ask. As we learned from 1 Samuel 16, only God sees the heart and knows for sure.

That's true also for our own confessions. What, if anything, do we bring to the light, and why? How can you tell the difference between a fake confession and a genuine one? How can we meaningfully repent of the larger systemic issues that we are part of?

WHEN FAITH MEANS RISK
JOHN 9:1-41

A few years ago, my mom and I traveled together to a family wedding in another province. Since she had trouble walking for any length of time, I suggested that we arrange for a wheelchair at the airport so she could save her strength to enjoy the wedding, and she agreed to try it. When we arrived at the airport, the staff had the wheelchair ready, the other passengers moved aside to let us pass, and we were even the first to board the plane. Everything went well, except that I noticed whenever people addressed us, they always talked with me and never to my mother. I couldn't help but wonder if that was because of the wheelchair—in part because it made her considerably lower than eye-level, and in part because people wrongly assumed that because she was in a wheelchair, she might not understand them. While people seemed to have good disability awareness in making allowances for the wheelchair, they somehow seemed less aware of the person in it.

In our Gospel text, Jesus encounters a man with a disability and responds to him in a much more natural way. Jesus *sees* the man. He doesn't ignore him. He doesn't express any reluctance to engage him. He doesn't talk more loudly or more slowly because the man can't see. He speaks with him person to person. He touches him. He heals him. Jesus recognizes the man's physical lack of eyesight, and also recognizes him as a person with parents, with a relationship to the Jewish synagogue and community, with an emotional and spiritual life in addition to his physical condition. — Mandie presiding @ Sikes funeral

When Jesus' disciples apparently assume that some sin had caused the man's blindness, Jesus corrects them and makes it clear that the man's blindness did not come from anything the man had done wrong or anything that his parents had done wrong. Instead, Jesus tells his disciples, "This happened so that God's mighty works might be displayed in him" (John 9:3). And Jesus goes on to demonstrate that by restoring the man's sight.

It takes just seven verses for Jesus to see the man, to make some mud and spread it on the man's eyes, and to have him wash in the pool of Siloam and then return miraculously able to see. What a wonderful, mighty work of God, just as Jesus had predicted. But that's not all. In the next thirty-one verses, God continues to work in this man's life so that he receives spiritual sight as well.

Immediately after his physical healing, the man can identify Jesus only as "the man they call Jesus" (verse 11). After being questioned by his neighbors and by the Pharisees, the man identifies Jesus as "a prophet" (verse 17). After the Pharisees talk with his parents and question him a second time, the man acknowledges that Jesus is "from God" (verse 33). And finally, after being expelled from the synagogue, and after Jesus himself searches him out again, the formerly blind man can say, "Lord, I believe" (verse 38). He finally sees that Jesus is not just another man, not just someone that "they" call Jesus. He now worships him as Jesus, the Lord of life.

The use of the word *know* in the course of the chapter highlights the man's growing spiritual insight. When the man's neighbors ask about the man who healed him, the formerly blind man says, "I don't *know*" where he is (verse 12). His parents say, "We *know* he is our son. We *know* he was born blind. But we don't *know* how he now sees, and we don't *know* who healed his eyes" (verses 20-21). The Pharisees say, "We *know* this man is a sinner," (verse 24), but the formerly blind man contradicts them saying, "I don't *know* whether he's a sinner" (verse 25).

Back and forth they go, until finally the man bursts out in exasperation, "This is incredible! You don't *know* where he is from, yet he healed my eyes! We *know* that God doesn't listen to sinners. . . . If this man wasn't from God, he couldn't do this" (verses 30-33). Throughout the chapter, the man grows in his knowledge of Jesus, even though it goes against what the Pharisees claim to know, even though his parents are afraid to say anything, even though it results in his being cut off from the synagogue. He takes a great risk in trusting Jesus, in worshiping him, and in discovering a new community of disciples.

One of the striking things about this text is that of the forty-one verses, Jesus appears only in the first seven verses when he restores the man's physical eyesight, and in the last seven verses after he hears that the man has been expelled from the synagogue. In the long middle section (verses 8-34), Jesus is absent as the formerly blind man talks with his neighbors, as he's questioned by the Pharisees, as his parents get involved, as he is turned out of the synagogue. Yet in spite of his absence, Jesus remains central to the story. "Where is he?" the people ask. Is he a sinner? Is he from God? For the man who received his sight and for every other person in this story, the real issue is how they "see" Jesus.

That's the issue for us today too. Whatever our physical ability to see or not see, whatever our abilities and disabilities, this text confronts us with the question: How do we see Jesus? With honesty and increasing knowledge like the man who had been born blind? With curiosity like the man who continues to grow in his understanding? With fear like his parents? With anger and threats like some of the religious leaders?

With risk-taking like the man himself? Jesus sees us physically and spiritually, where we need healing and where we have already begun to grow and change. How do we see Jesus?

The man who had been born blind risks his relationship with his parents and with the wider community represented by the synagogue. What risks do you face today in believing and worshiping Jesus?

Psalm 23

1 The LORD is my shepherd.
   I lack nothing.
2 He lets me rest in grassy meadows;
   he leads me to restful waters;
3   he keeps me alive.
He guides me in proper paths
   for the sake of his good name.
4 Even when I walk through the darkest valley,
   I fear no danger because you are with me.
Your rod and your staff—
   they protect me.
5 You set a table for me
   right in front of my enemies.
You bathe my head in oil;
   my cup is so full it spills over!
6 Yes, goodness and faithful love
   will pursue me all the days of my life,
   and I will live in the LORD's house
   as long as I live.

GROUP STUDY GUIDE

Questions for Discussion

1. In the Old Testament text for this week, Samuel appears initially reluctant to obey God's word. What convinces him to follow through? Reflect on a similar experience of your own. How did you resolve your misgivings?

2. In 1 Samuel 16, Jesse does not include David when he introduces each of his sons to Samuel. Why might Jesse have overlooked or deliberately skipped over David? What did you do the last time you felt overlooked or inadequate for a particular situation or task?

3. This week's commentary introduces the Ephesians text in the setting of baptism or confirmation. How might these verses also apply to more seasoned Christians?

4. In our Gospel text, the man's spiritual rebirth takes almost all of John 9 as he grows in his understanding of Jesus. Create a personal timeline of your spiritual journey from your first awareness of God to the present. What have you been learning along the way? Or if you're at the beginning of your journey, what do you hope to learn?

5. In addition to the main focus on Jesus' identity, John 9 raises a number of other issues. At the very beginning of the text, Jesus' disciples ask what caused this man's blindness: Was it his sin or the sin of his parents? The Pharisees raise the issue of keeping the Sabbath: If Jesus is really from God, how can he do the work of healing on the Sabbath day of rest that God had commanded? Others question whether the man was really the same blind man who used to sit by the road and beg: Perhaps this was some kind of hoax or case of mistaken identity. Sin, Sabbath, and healing occur repeatedly throughout the Gospel of John. Choose one of these themes, and use a concordance to explore it further. What is the importance of sin, Sabbath, or healing in John's Gospel, and what do these themes communicate to us about Jesus Christ?

Suggestions for Group Study

Coloring Time

Many children enjoy coloring as a quiet activity, and now adults are rediscovering coloring to express creativity, reduce stress, and have some fun. For some, coloring can also be a form of prayer as they meditate and listen to God. Look online for one of the many free Scripture coloring pages, print out copies for your group, and bring colored pencils or pens to share. As you color, pay particular attention to *chiaroscuro,* the interplay between light and dark. Which portions will you make darker, lighter, or leave uncolored, and why? What does it mean for God to be "light"?

Hymn Writing

Ephesians 5:14 ends with a quotation that may have been taken from an ancient hymn: "Wake up, sleeper! Get up from the dead, and Christ will shine on you." Write several more lines of the hymn using words drawn from other parts of the Ephesians text. For example, the next line could be: "Children of light, arise! May your fruit be good and just and true." Or maybe: "Let Christ shine bright, and live in God's light." Write one or several verses with the words from Ephesians as the opening line. Or think of the words from Ephesians as the refrain and write several verses to go with it. Feel free to rhyme or not as you choose. Vary the style between traditional hymn, worship chorus, rap, or other musical form.

Closing Prayer

O God of light, we come to you as your children who bear your image. We are children of light, and yet, we often fail to reflect your light and life. Release us from any dark thoughts that might bind us—from any fear, anxiety, anger, or misplaced desires. Reorient our actions toward those things that are faithful and life-giving. Through Jesus Christ, we receive your forgiveness and grace. Through your Spirit, we receive new inspiration and power. Grant us new eyes to see your work in us and all around us. Grant us new eyes to see you as Healer, Good Shepherd, Guide, and Lord of Life. We worship you. Amen.

Waiting for Resurrection

Scriptures for the
Fifth Sunday of Lent
Ezekiel 37:1-14
Romans 8:6-11
John 11:1-45

This week's texts focus so much on Resurrection that we might almost wonder if Lent had ended while we weren't looking. Easter and the death and resurrection of Jesus are still to come, yet the resurrection power of God bursts out in both the Old and New Testaments. It functions as the overarching theme of all four Scripture readings designated for this week, even as we still wait for the final resurrection to come.

In the Book of Ezekiel, the Spirit of God sets the prophet in a valley full of dry bones and asks, "Can these bones live again?" (verse 3). Ezekiel hardly knows what to say, and relies on God to answer: "The Lord God proclaims to these bones: I am about to put breath in you, and you will live again" (verse 5). As Ezekiel speaks the word of God over the dry bones, they suddenly come to life bone by bone, sinew by sinew, with flesh and skin, breathed into life by the breath of the Spirit.

Our Romans text contrasts a life based on selfishness with a life based on the Spirit. On the one hand, selfishness means hostility to God and leads to sin and death. On the other, the life of the Spirit means peace and a life pleasing to God. The text ends with a reference to the resurrection of Jesus. Just as the Spirit of God raised Jesus from the dead, God gives life to us through that same Spirit. The resurrection power of God can transform our lives in practical, daily living.

Jesus claims that same power to the glory of God in John 11. When he first receives the message that Lazarus is ill, Jesus waits two days before he returns to Bethany where Lazarus lives with his two sisters.

Why would he go back at all, his disciples wondered, when some were ready to stone him? When he finally arrives, both Martha and Mary reproach him: "Lord, if you had been here, my brother wouldn't have died" (verse 21, 32). In answer to their spoken and unspoken questions, Jesus asks a question of his own: "Didn't I tell you that if you believe, you will see God's glory?" (verse 40, compare verse 4). With that, Jesus offers a brief prayer, and then to everyone's surprise, he calls Lazarus out of the tomb.

Even the psalm for this week hints at resurrection, as Psalm 130 begins with a plea for God's mercy: "I cry out to you from the depths, LORD—my Lord, listen to my voice!" (verses 1-2). But this confessional tone almost immediately gives way to words of assurance: "If you kept track of sins, LORD—my Lord, who would stand a chance? But forgiveness is with you" (verses 3-4). From there, the Psalm goes on to speak of hope, of God's faithful love and redemption from sin. God's resurrection means release from despair, and a new way of life with God's hope and mercy.

So this week as we continue with Lent, we do so with our sights set firmly on the resurrection to come. May the same Spirit that raised Jesus from the dead and brought new life to Lazarus and to dry, dead bones, be the same Spirit that blows new life into us today.

DEM DRY BONES
EZEKIEL 37:1-14

When I introduced this Ezekiel text to my small group, several broke out singing spontaneously, "Dem bones, dem bones, dem dry bones, Dem bones, dem bones, dem dry bones, Dem bones, dem bones, dem dry bones, Now hear the word of the Lord." The catchy tune of the African American spiritual made the rest of us smile as several others started tapping their feet and swaying to the rhythm. What I considered a rather gruesome vision given to the prophet became instantly less frightening. I had imagined Ezekiel's gloomy valley with the dead rising like ghastly, ghostly figures, like zombies from the horror movies I never watch. But in that moment of light-hearted song those figures became humorous and almost comical.

In contrast, the original setting of this text was certainly no laughing matter. Ezekiel's people lived in exile away from their homeland in circumstances that seemed hopeless. A survivor of the destruction of Jerusalem told Ezekiel, "The city has fallen!" (33:21). The people of Jerusalem and Judah were broken and scattered. They were Ezekiel's valley of dry bones—a great crowd of people once full of life, now devastated by exile and drained of every ounce of energy. Dead, dry, and disconnected, they had no vitality of their own, no way to pull themselves together and be the community they once were.

Could they live again? It seemed impossible, a reality underscored by Ezekiel's observation that the bones were "very dry" (verse 2). They gave no sign of life. But in Ezekiel's divinely inspired vision, the resurrection power of God raises them to new life! For Ezekiel's people, his vision was neither gruesome nor comical. His vision radiated hope for their future.

In Ezekiel's vision, new life began with the word of God. "Prophesy over these bones," the Lord said. "Dry bones, hear the LORD's word!" (verse 4). So Ezekiel prophesied over them just as God directed him, and the dry, dead bones responded. With a great noise and shaking, the bones came together. As the old song goes, "the toe bone connected to the foot bone, the foot bone connected to the heel bone," and so on, until a vast army stood in that valley. The scene mirrored the creation account of Genesis 1, where God spoke and created the entire universe and everything in it. Now here in Ezekiel's vision, God spoke again and recreated life.

As I began writing this chapter, I listened to the Delta River Boys' version of "Dem Bones," which includes the often-repeated line "Now hear the word of the Lord." It comes at the end of the first verse, repeats throughout the song, and gives the finishing touch to the song's finale. That the song gives such prominence to hearing the word of the Lord reflects our text where God's word is clearly central to the story. But when I checked out other versions of the song online, I noticed that several had omitted the word of the Lord altogether. In the hands of a variety of different editors, "Now hear the word of the Lord" had become "Dem noisy, dry bones," or "And that's the way it goes," or "Doin' the skeleton dance," or even "Let's shake them skeleton bones," some with animated skeletons apparently doing a happy dance. Perhaps these versions satisfied their editors' purposes, but I missed that ringing affirmation, "Now hear the word of the Lord."

After all, without the word of the Lord, Ezekiel would have received no instruction, and the valley of bones would have remained still and silent. Without the word of the Lord, there would have been no bone connecting with bone, no new flesh, no new life, and certainly no dancing. Just as in the creation account of Genesis 1, so here in Ezekiel 37, the word of the Lord played a critical role and set everything in motion.

Next the Lord said to Ezekiel, "Prophesy to the breath. . . . The Lord God proclaims: Come from the four winds, breath! Breathe into these dead bodies and let them live" (verse 9). Again, Ezekiel prophesied according to God's word, and the breath entered the bodies, gave them new life, and caused them to stand. The Hebrew word *ruah* occurs ten times in our text, translated variously as breath, wind, and Spirit. Just as God breathed life into the first human being in Genesis 2, so here God caused breath to bring new life.

What God's word began, the Spirit of God continued to completion. "Can these bones live again?" (verse 3). Ezekiel could now answer, Yes! Yes! Yes! By the resurrection power of God, these bones lived again! "Ezekiel connected dem dry bones," sang the Delta Rhythm Boys, but more accurately, it was the Lord God who connected the dry bones in Ezekiel's vision. By word and Spirit, the Creator of all things created new life once again. As a prophet, Ezekiel was "in the LORD's spirit" (verse 1), but he did not gather up the bones and connect them by his own efforts. Instead, he served as a faithful witness who received God's vision and then proclaimed it.

Ezekiel's vision ended with a word from God addressed directly to his people. As if to reinforce the vision of dry bones coming to life, God said, "I'm opening your graves! I will raise you up from your graves, my people, and I will bring you to Israel's fertile land. . . . I will put my breath in you, and you will live" (verses 12, 14). One day their long exile would be over. One day they would return home with joy and purpose. One day they would feel fully alive once more as a community of God's people.

Like Ezekiel and his people, our world today could use a fresh vision of hope. We have our own valleys of bones, from the killing fields of Cambodia to the mass graves of Chechnya and Iraq to the many, many more victims of violence and oppression around the world. "Can these dry bones live?" we might well ask. Can fallen and disconnected communities be restored? Is Ezekiel's vision for us too?

As you look at your community and world, what "dry bones" can you identify that appear disconnected and impossible to put back together and regenerate? Where do you see signs of new life?

LIFE IN THE SPIRIT
ROMANS 8:6-11

The Boy Who Came Back from Heaven was the story of a six-year-old boy who had barely survived a terrible car accident. Alex had a severely injured spine and brain trauma, and he lay in a coma for two months. When he eventually woke up, he told his parents that he had died and gone to heaven. He had seen angels and talked with Jesus. His story, coauthored with his father, became a best-selling book and went on to sell over a million copies. Five years after its publication, however, Alex publicly retracted the story. In an open letter to sellers, buyers, and promoters, he wrote, "I did not die. I did not go to Heaven. I said I went to heaven because I thought it would get me attention."

The publisher withdrew the book, but I can't help wondering why it took so long for that to happen, since Alex had started disavowing the story several years earlier. How did his parents' relationship fit into the picture, with Alex's dad as the sole copyright owner of the book and Alex's mother helping her son to disavow it? And what of the little boy himself who had been severely injured and understandably in need of attention, whose story was exploited in such a big way, who has grown up since then but still seems caught between his estranged parents? My heart goes out to Alex and his sad story.

Alex's story also makes me wonder, what is the purpose of resurrection? For anyone miraculously blessed with a new lease on life, what comes next? Is the next step to write a book that gets attention and sells a million copies, as with Alex's near-death experience? Does resurrection mean having a second chance at life, an opportunity to live more fully and thankfully than ever before? In the words of Jesus, the raising of Lazarus meant honor and glory to God. When Jesus heard that his friend had fallen ill, he said, "This illness isn't fatal. It's for the glory of God so that God's Son can be glorified through it" (John 11:4). And just before Jesus raised Lazarus from the dead, he said to Martha, "Didn't I tell you that if you believe, you will see God's glory?" (John 11:40). As just one example of the resurrection power of God, the raising of Lazarus gave God the glory, and it functioned as a testimony that called Martha, Mary, and many others to believe in Jesus (John 11:42, 45).

If all that weren't enough, our text from Romans 8 expands further on the meaning and purpose of the resurrection. Our lectionary verses form just one part of Paul's discussion on the great themes of the Christian faith that take up the first eleven chapters of his letter: sin, righteousness, God's faithfulness and justice, the role of the Law, the new freedom we have in Christ, and much more. As we have already seen in Romans 5, Adam and Christ represent two ways of life: the old way of sin and death, and the new way of forgiveness and life in Jesus Christ. Our text from Romans extends that now as it contrasts the way of selfishness and the way of the Spirit.

On the one side, the attitude of selfishness is self-centered, incapable of submitting to God's law, unable to please God, and results in death. On the other side is the attitude that comes from the Spirit, that's characterized by God's righteousness, that leads to life and peace. For Paul, the critical difference between the two is the resurrection of Christ. In verse 11, his logic goes like this: If Christ has been raised from the dead, and if the same Spirit that raised him now lives in us, we, too, can live a new life. By the death and resurrection of Jesus, we are set free from Adam, sin, and death, and we are set free to life in the Spirit.

That's the meaning and purpose of resurrection—not as a one-time only historical fact of Jesus long ago, and not as an individual, personal miracle to draw attention to ourselves, but as a new way of life for all who believe, a new attitude and mindset that transforms every area of life. Since Christ is raised from the dead, since we have Christ's life in us, we live a new life by his Spirit. What Ezekiel shared as a future vision for God's people, what the Gospel of John demonstrated in Jesus' raising of Lazarus, the apostle Paul describes in his own uniquely theological expression.

Paul continues his theological discussion until the end of Romans 11, where he concludes with a hymn of praise for God's riches and wisdom: "All things are from him and through him and for him. May the glory be to him forever. Amen" (Romans 11:36). Then in the remaining chapters of the book, he speaks more practically about what this new life in the Spirit means for the Roman church in the form of changed lives and relationships. By the grace of God, they will exercise their various spiritual gifts, love and honor one another, welcome strangers, bless those who persecute them, do what's right, fulfill their debts, be patient with one another, serve the Lord, pray and work together. Paul paints a beautiful picture of the transformed, Spirit-led, unselfish church. That's what it meant for the Roman church to live out the resurrection, to live in the Spirit, and that's what it means for us today.

That's the kind of unselfish, Spirit-led community that I would want to belong to, and the kind of community that many in the world are hungry for today—men and women, of any age and culture. Humanly speaking, we're not entirely there yet. As individuals and as a church, we don't always love one another as we should; we get impatient; we flag in our enthusiasm for serving the Lord. Life in the Spirit seems to elude us time and time again. "But you aren't self-centered," Paul says confidently (verse 9). Even now, the Spirit of God is within us and giving us new life.

How can you explain the discrepancy between Paul's statement "you aren't self-centered" and the self-centeredness that seems so evident in our own lives and in the church? Where do you see evidence of unselfishness?

WAITING AND WEEPING
JOHN 11:1-45

At a recent memorial service at my church, the family followed the Chinese custom of giving each person a small envelope as a sign of respect and gratitude for their presence. The envelopes were white—the color of mourning—and inside was a candy, because death tastes bitter, mourning can be hard work, and now we need something sweet.

Printed on one side of the envelope was a cross with Easter lilies as a reminder of Jesus' suffering, death, and resurrection. On the other side, written in Chinese characters, was John 11:25: "I am the resurrection and the life. Whoever believes in me will live, even though they die." What fitting words, for they represented our dear sister's Christian faith and conviction. What's more, they served as an invitation and a promise to each one of us to believe in Jesus and receive new life.

In their original setting, these words of affirmation come about mid-way in our Gospel text, as Jesus;' words of comfort to Martha on the death of her brother, Lazarus. When Jesus first arrived at their home in Bethany, Martha couldn't help but blurt out, "Lord, if you had been here, my brother wouldn't have died" (verse 21). When her sister, Mary, saw Jesus, she reproached him with the same words: "Lord, if you had been here, my brother wouldn't have died" (verse 32). The two sisters and their brother had believed in Jesus and were among his closest friends. But if Jesus were truly the resurrection and the life, why then didn't he save Lazarus?

Mary and Martha hadn't exactly asked Jesus to come to them in Bethany. Their message in verse 3 of our text was simply: "Lord, the one whom you love is ill." As close friends of Jesus, they were quite likely aware that Jesus' life was in danger. Time and again, as Jesus taught on the Temple grounds in Jerusalem, the people became so angry that they wanted to stone him (John 8:59; 10:31-39). So Jesus had withdrawn from Jerusalem to the area of the Jordan River, withdrawn from the threats on his life to a place of relative safety, for "many believed in Jesus there" (John 10:42).

Mary and Martha must have been glad that he was safe. They wouldn't have wanted to endanger him, and perhaps that's why they didn't make a direct request for him to come. Yet from their identical responses, both sisters had clearly been hoping and waiting for him. Instead of leaving immediately to help them, however, Jesus stayed where he was for two more days.

In his defense, by the time that Jesus received the message from Mary and Martha that Lazarus was sick, it was quite likely that Lazarus had already died. After all, by the time Jesus finally arrived in Bethany, Lazarus had already been dead and buried for four days. Working backwards on the timeline, if it took Jesus one day's journey from the Jordan River area to Bethany, and if he stayed where he was for two days after receiving the message from the two sisters, and if those who brought the message took one day's journey from Bethany to find him, that makes four days.

So Lazarus quite likely died shortly after the messengers had gone out to find Jesus.

But the question still remains. Why did Jesus wait? Even if Lazarus had already died, why didn't Jesus leave immediately to comfort Mary and Martha, and cut short their mourning?

In John 2 at a wedding in Cana, Jesus' mother said to him, "They don't have any wine." Just like Mary and Martha in our story, Jesus' mother did not make a direct request. Yet just like the two sisters, she clearly expected Jesus to act. But Jesus waited until finally, later in the story, he changed the water into wine for the wedding guests. In John 7, Jesus' brothers urged him to go to Judea for the Jewish Festival of Booths. But Jesus stayed in Galilee—he waited—until finally, later in the story, he went to the festival after the others had already left.

Now here in our text, Jesus receives this message from Mary and Martha . . . and he waits. In all three stories, he waits until the time is right, until God's purpose and God's way is clear. In this particular story, he says, "it's for the glory of God" (verse 4), "so that you can believe" (verse 15), "so that they will believe" (verse 42) that God had sent him.

When things go wrong, when I find myself waiting and waiting and waiting for God to act, I want to believe that God has a purpose that is beyond my limited understanding. I tell myself that God is sovereign and won't be pushed into doing something before the time is right. I don't have a puppet god who will do whatever I want or whatever you want. Or who can be bribed or manipulated or threatened or coerced. God has a greater purpose beyond what we can see and know.

But I also have a good deal of Martha and Mary in me. Just as they reproached Jesus in their grief, I also wonder: Lord, if you had been in Syria and Congo and around the world, people wouldn't be suffering as refugees. If you—the One who stilled the storms—had been in the Philippines and Japan and around the world, people wouldn't be devastated by hurricanes and tsunamis. Where is your good will and way for the millions who have died in violence and war, from hunger, disease, and lack of clean water? Why is the world still waiting for resurrection and new life when you have the power to give it now?

As Mary, Martha, and Lazarus waited for Jesus, as Jesus didn't come at first and Lazarus died, as his sisters buried him and mourned his loss, they too were waiting for resurrection. In the end, everything worked together for good, even Jesus' delay, as Jesus miraculously raised Lazarus from the dead and restored him with joy to his two sisters. It took a long time to get there; for most of the story, all they had was hurt and hope. But they did not hope and hurt alone. Jesus came and wept with them (verse 35). Jesus also waits and weeps with us.

Jesus says to Martha, "Everyone who lives and believes in me will never die. Do you believe this?" (verse 26). On a scale of 1 to 10 with 1 being disbelief and 10 being full belief, what answer would you give to Jesus' question? What difference might believing or disbelieving make to your daily life?

Psalm 130

¹ I cry out to you from the depths, LORD—
² my Lord, listen to my voice!
   Let your ears pay close attention to my request for mercy!
³ If you kept track of sins, LORD—
   my Lord, who would stand a chance?
⁴ But forgiveness is with you—
   that's why you are honored.
⁵ I hope, LORD.
My whole being hopes,
   and I wait for God's promise.
⁶ My whole being waits for my Lord—
   more than the night watch waits for morning;
   yes, more than the night watch waits for morning!
⁷ Israel, wait for the LORD!
   Because faithful love is with the LORD;
   because great redemption is with our God!
⁸ He is the one who will redeem Israel from all its sin.

GROUP STUDY GUIDE

Questions for Discussion

1. A member of my small group summarized the meaning of Ezekiel's vision with these words: "God breathes new life into the most desperate situations." What desperate situations can you identify in your life and in the world? What would new life look like in those contexts?

2. Romans 8 warns against self-centeredness in favor of life in the Spirit. But isn't a little selfishness appropriate at times? After all, as some might argue, if you don't love yourself, you can't love anyone else. If you don't take care of yourself first, you can't take care of anyone else. It's like the airplane safety talk: If the oxygen masks come down, first put on your own mask before helping your child or anyone else. How can you discern the difference between good self-care that enables us to care for others and the selfishness that Romans describes?

3. For each character in John 11, identify how each one responds to the death of Lazarus. Note how the responses of Martha and Mary differ and how they are similar. How does Jesus respond, and how does his response change throughout the story? Reflect on your own experiences of grief, identify your different responses, and receive God's comfort.

4. In John 11:25, Jesus says, "I am the resurrection and the life." Centuries earlier, when God called Moses to lead the people out of Egypt, God revealed the divine name as "I Am." Here in the Gospel of John, Jesus uses the same "I Am" language to identify himself. How many "I Am" statements can you identify in the Gospel, with or without a concordance? How do these different statements help to round out your understanding of Jesus' identity?

5. The four lectionary texts this week speak of resurrection in four different ways: (1) the dream-like quality of Ezekiel's vision, (2) the theological reflection of Romans, (3) the narrative of John's Gospel, and (4) the poetry of the Psalm. To which genre do you respond most easily? Which do you find more difficult to grasp? How does each contribute to a deeper understanding of resurrection?

Suggestions for Group Study

Make a Prayer List

Make a prayer list of those you know who are ill and/or have recently lost a loved one. Does God seem to be delaying in some way? Where can you see glimpses of God's glory? Offer prayers for healing, comfort, and continued trust in God. Brainstorm ways of showing that you care, like making and sending cards, sending an e-mail, taking flowers, or some other thoughtful gesture. Then pick one or more and follow through.

Explore Wendell Berry's Poem

Look up Wendell Berry's poem, "Manifesto: The Mad Farmer Liberation Front," and read it together. Note the last line of the poem, "Practice resurrection." What examples does he give throughout his poem? Do you agree that these are examples of practicing resurrection? Why or why not? Make your own list of practicing resurrection.

Closing Prayer

For the resurrection power of God, we give thanks and praise! By your Spirit, breathe new life into our ordinary days. Reorient us from any self-centeredness to find our new center in Jesus. Fill us and empower us with resurrection life to glorify your name, to love and honor others, to use whatever gifts you have given us for the common good. For those who are sick, we pray for your healing touch to remove any pain, to bring clarity in any treatment decisions, to strengthen faith, to bring peace in the midst of uncertainty. For those who have lost loved ones, we pray for your grace to mourn well, that they may be surrounded by many who offer comfort and support, that they may know your peace that passes all understanding. To you, the Lord of life, we offer our prayers and wait on you. Amen.

The Passion of the Christ

Scriptures for the
Sixth Sunday of Lent
Isaiah 50:4-9a
Philippians 2:5-11
Matthew 27:11-54

Every year, I relive Holy Week with my congregation in worship, from the children waving palm branches on Palm Sunday while the rest of us sing "Hosanna;" to our dimly lit Thursday evening Communion in remembrance of Jesus' last supper with his disciples; to his crucifixion and death on Good Friday remembered in a joint service with other churches; to placing flowers on the cross on Easter Sunday as a sign of his resurrection. "But isn't that a lot of work to have so many services?" a friend from another church asked. "Do people really want to be in church that much?

Well, yes, as much as I try to spread out the various responsibilities, Holy Week can seem like a lot of work, and no, not everyone participates in every service. But many do, and for me personally, the movement of that last week of Jesus' life has become a significant part of my own spiritual journey. At different points in my life, I've also felt welcomed and supported by others; I've had my share of critics, and I've had my lonely nights when I've felt abandoned. None of this has been to the point of arrest and execution like Jesus, but it's enough to identify with the events of the last week of his life. My journey with Jesus during Holy Week reminds me that Jesus journeys with me through all of the ups and downs of my life.

To my surprise, the lectionary texts designated for this week skip over Palm Sunday in favor of Passion Sunday. Forget the triumphal entry into the city of Jerusalem. Forget the palm branches and cries of "hosanna!" Our Matthew text for this week begins with Jesus already arrested and standing before Pilate. From there, the narrative moves relentlessly onward to the cries of the crowd and Pilate's decision to hand Jesus over for execution, to Jesus being tortured and crucified, to the taunting of passersby and his final, agonizing death. The earth shakes in response to the death of Jesus, and the curtain of the sanctuary is torn in two (Matthew 27:51).

In a similar vein, the other readings for this week also lean more toward passion and suffering than the celebration of Palm Sunday. Isaiah 50:4-9a speaks in the voice of one who has suffered in silence and who looks to God for help. Psalm 31 offers a desperate prayer for mercy and deliverance from an unspecified grief. Philippians 2:5-11 speaks directly of Christ Jesus who "emptied himself" (verse 7) to become human and submit to death on the cross. As we enter this last week of Lent, we enter into Jesus' passion. The last hosannas of Palm Sunday have fallen silent, and Jesus' triumphal entry into Jerusalem has already faded to black.

GOD'S FAITHFUL SERVANT
ISAIAH 50:4-9a

The Book of Isaiah includes four servant songs with the following titles in the Common English Bible: (1) "God's servant described" (42:1-4); (2) "The servant speaks up" (49:1-6); (3) "God's faithful servant" (50:4-9); (4) "Suffering servant" (52:13–53:12). Taken together, they form a picture of God's chosen servant, filled by the Spirit to bring justice, who speaks on God's behalf, but who suffers grave insult and affliction. The servant meant to bring justice suffers an unjust death.

In the third of these songs, designated as the Old Testament text for this week, the words "the LORD God" appear four times in just six verses. This constant focus on God runs like a thread throughout the passage to tie it together. In verse 4, the servant wakes up in the morning and learns from the LORD God before speaking a word of encouragement to other weary souls. In verse 5, the servant listens to the LORD God without rebelling or turning away. Even when beaten and abused, the servant doesn't withdraw from God, but says in verse 7, "The LORD God will help me," and again in verse 9, "The LORD God will help me." The repetition reinforces the thought. The servant's relationship with God endures even through great difficulty.

In this text, the servant's confidence in God remains unshaken even as he endures beating, mocking, and spitting. No matter what happens, no matter who his accusers are or how many, the servant does not retaliate in kind, but relies instead on God's help. The LORD's protection is so great, that even when the servant is insulted, he says, it's as if "I haven't been insulted" (verse 7). Others may torment him, but he remains safe with God. Others may accuse and condemn him, but he continues to cling to God as his help.

Elsewhere, the Book of Isaiah identifies Israel as God's servant (41:8). After all, the people of Israel were God's chosen people, and certainly they had suffered throughout their history—from their years of slavery in Egypt, to their homelessness in the wilderness, to civil war and the attack of foreign powers, to their eventual exile from their Promised Land. Through it all, God had remained faithful, saving them time and time again. They still remained God's people. Like the servant of Isaiah 50, they could rely on God's help.

From the vantage point of the New Testament, we may also see Jesus as the suffering servant. After his arrest, Jesus suffered beating, mocking, and spitting (Matthew 27:27-31). Yet for all the abuse he endured, he too never retaliated in kind. When the guards came with swords to arrest him, and when a servant of the high priest got his ear cut off in the skirmish, Jesus cried out, "Stop! No more of this!" and he healed the man's ear (Luke 22:51). Even on the cross, Jesus prayed for his tormentors, "Father, forgive them, for they don't know what they're doing" (Luke 23:34). Through everything he suffered, Jesus remained God's faithful servant.

For those who suffer insult and injury today, the suffering servant of Isaiah offers hope and comfort. As the first two servant songs make clear, God wills justice and will not rest until justice has been established (Isaiah 42:1-4; 49:4). Today, we're still waiting for God to bring justice—for those kept in poverty by unjust systems and attitudes; for Indigenous people, African Americans, and other racial minorities; for equal pay for equal work regardless of gender; for justice between nations. We're still waiting, and God is still at work! Now here in the third servant song, God helps the servant who is unjustly attacked, and many today still wait for that as well. God, have mercy. Lord, have mercy.

As I read myself into this text, I also note the servant's intimate relationship with God, and I long for that same deep trust and confidence. The servant remained close even in the face of suffering. Perhaps he questioned why he was being attacked. He may have wondered why God didn't do more to end his suffering. At that point, he may have found it difficult to read Scripture or even to pray. But instead of cutting himself off from a relationship with God, he held on. Instead of ending his faith, he allowed his suffering to deepen it. And if we can do the same—to hold on to God when everything around us and in us says to let go—if we can remain in relationship with God instead of drawing back, then our trust and confidence in God may also deepen.

The servant in our text began his day with listening: "God awakens my ear in the morning to listen, as educated people do" (verse 4). Today that might mean listening to God by reading Scripture, or going for a walk, or simply sitting silently in God's presence. I often light a candle and journal early in the morning, listening for God's voice that way. At night, I keep a simple gratitude list of five things that I appreciate about my day. Other ways of listening to God might include reading a good book, praying the Lord's prayer, playing or listening to music, periodic fasting from food or social media, reading or writing poetry. For the servant in our text, listening to God provided the foundation for his justice work and for the words of encouragement he would speak to others. Today, too, our listening to God enables us to act, speak, and persevere through suffering. Whether you're a morning person, a night owl, or somewhere in between, whatever time works best for you, whatever form of listening you choose, daily listening to God can help nurture your faith, guide your words and actions, and strengthen your confidence in the One who helps us.

In our text, verse 4 refers to the word that sustains the weary. What words help to sustain you when you are weary? Who do you know that is weary, and what, if anything, might you say to them?

HUMILITY INFUSED WITH HOPE
PHILIPPIANS 2:5-11

Paul planted the Philippian church on his second missionary journey, so he knew the people well. As a young church, they had supported him in his ministry both financially and by their prayers. They gave him deep joy as he says in the first part of his letter (Philippians 1:3-4), but they also faced some challenges as they struggled to remain faithful (Philippians 1:27-30) and as two leaders struggled with a disagreement (Philippians 4:2-3). As the founding apostle, Paul writes this letter to encourage and advise all of them. "Adopt the attitude that was in Christ Jesus," he says (Philippians 2:5). Then to illustrate what he means, he cites a hymn which forms the majority of our reading.

The first half of the hymn (verses 6-8) speaks of Jesus' humility. The dictionary definition of humility includes being respectful, humble, lowly, meek, modest. The word itself appears so meek and modest, that there seem to be many more definitions for what humility is not: Humility is not arrogance, pride, egotism, superiority; It's not conceited, lofty, presumptuous, or pretentious. Humility is the opposite of all those things.

Jesus showed humility throughout his life and death. Although he was "equal with God" (verse 6), he set that aside to live in humble circumstances as a human being. A feed trough for animals served as his first bed. Shepherds—who were at the bottom end of the social ladder—were among his first visitors. As a grown man, Jesus entered the building trade like his earthly father, but soon became an itinerant preacher and teacher, spending time with fishermen, tax collectors, prostitutes, and other ordinary folk. When he entered Jerusalem for the last time, he rode on a humble donkey. At the end of his life, he was arrested, questioned, tortured, and executed like a common criminal. Yet he did not retaliate, or demand justice, or call down legions of angels to defend himself. Jesus had set aside divinity to take on humanity, "to the point of death, even death on a cross" (verse 8).

If that were the whole story of Jesus, he might be a man to be pitied more than anything else—a man who had his 15 minutes of fame, but who otherwise lived in relative obscurity, a victim of the political establishment of his time, too weak and too ignorant to speak up and fight the system, a lonely and pathetic figure instead of an inspiration. But the humility of Jesus makes up just one side of the story and just one part of the hymn that Paul cites here in Philippians. While the first half of the hymn spotlights Jesus' humility, the last half of the hymn is all about his glory.

God highly honored Jesus with a name greater than all other names, which would cause everyone to bow before him and confess that "Jesus Christ is Lord" (verse 11). Jesus was not only a man of humble circumstances who died a lowly death. He was not only a good teacher long ago. He was and is Jesus Christ, the Lord of everyone and everything. The glory of God that he had given up to become a human being still belongs to him and is revealed once more.

Glimpses of that glory could be seen even in his earthly life. Although Jesus was born in a stable, his birth was announced by angels, and he received precious gifts of gold, myrrh, and frankincense, all fit for a king. Throughout his ministry as an adult, he performed miracles, healing people from disease and even raising people from the dead. One day when he was praying with three of his disciples, he was transformed and bathed in the bright light of heavenly glory (Matthew 17:1-8). So while Jesus' life was characterized by humility, hints of his glory also shone through.

Given this picture of Jesus in his full humanity and full divine glory, what does it mean to have the same attitude as Christ Jesus? How were the Philippians to live in light of Jesus' humility and glory? And what might it mean for us today?

We might be tempted to limit humility as an inner quality of being modest, of being respectful, of not being proud. But humility has a relational quality as well. For people who are struggling with one another, humility means speaking gently instead of using harsh words; giving others the benefit of the doubt; being able to admit when you're wrong; saying "I'm sorry;" giving and receiving forgiveness. Humility means being unselfish (2:3), thinking more about what's good for others than about ourselves (2:4). In Christian community, humility is not only for those who are already lowly in terms of their social status, but a relational posture meant for all. "In your relationships with one another, have the same mindset as Christ Jesus" (verse 5, emphasis added) as the New International Version puts it. Whatever the details of the Philippians' struggle with one another, an attitude of humility would be transformative.

While the Philippians were to follow Jesus in relating to one another in humility as fellow human beings, Paul reminded them that Jesus also reigned as their risen and glorious Savior. They had a future hope! Whatever their complaints and disagreements with one another might be, they had this future hope in common. Whatever trials they might face in this life, they could look beyond their present conflict to their hope in God. So besides an inward and outward humility, they could have an inward and outward confidence in the way they related to one another.

For us, too, in whatever challenges we face today, humility and hope in God can go hand in hand. As human beings, we don't have all of the answers to our problems. We make mistakes; we may disagree with one another and hurt one another. So humility is certainly in order. But as followers of Jesus, we have a Savior who walks with us, who died for us to bring forgiveness and new life, who now reigns in glory and gives us hope beyond ourselves. So our present humility can be infused with hope, and our visions for the future tempered with humility. Let us then have the same attitude as Christ Jesus.

Are you drawn more naturally to humility or to visions of glory? How do both of these play out in your personal relationships?

SAVIOR OF THE WORLD
MATTHEW 27:11-54

"Passion" conveys a strong emotion, a powerful feeling for something that leads to action. A teacher with a passion for his students spends long hours preparing lesson plans, pays for supplies out of his own salary, and because some of the children regularly come to school hungry, he makes sure he has food available for them every day. An artist passionate about art and community building organizes joint art projects that bring together women on the street, the university women's club, and other women in the community. In his earthly life, Jesus had such passion for God that he gave his life to preaching, teaching, and healing, which eventually led to his arrest, suffering, and death.

That's one way of understanding Jesus' passion—as a powerful, God-given inner drive that compelled him to action and caused his opponents to have him executed. But the word "passion" comes from the Latin word *passio,* which means suffering or enduring. So the "passion" of Christ speaks more specifically of his suffering, especially the final events of his life. In that sense, our Gospel text for today is Matthew's retelling of Jesus' passion, from his trial and sentence before Pilate to his death on the cross. Jesus suffered and endured until the end. —➔ scripture

When Jesus appeared before Pilate, the governor asked, "Are you the king of the Jews?" (verse 11). Instead of answering directly, Jesus turned Pilate's own words against him and replied, "That's what you say" (verse 11). As Pilate continued to question him, Jesus fell silent. When the soldiers mocked him and beat him, they jeeringly addressed him as "King of the Jews" (verse 29), and again, Jesus did not reply. Instead, the Roman authorities unwittingly confessed to the truth when they posted a sign above Jesus' head as he hung on the cross. On it, they meant to write the charge that condemned him to death, but the words testified to much more: "This is Jesus, the king of the Jews" (verse 37). — who are you - Identity - belonging

The dispute over Jesus' identity as the King of the Jews ran parallel to the dispute over his identity as the Son of God. When the high priest demanded, "tell us whether you are the Christ, God's Son" (Matthew 26:63), instead of answering directly, Jesus replied, "You said it" (Matthew 26:64), turning the high priest's own words against him. Then as he hung on the cross and passersby taunted, "If you are God's Son, come down from the cross" (Matthew 27:40), he did not reply. His only words were a cry of agony to God. But in the end—in light of Jesus' suffering and death, in light of the violent earthquake that marked his sacrifice—the centurion and other guards supplied the testimony: "This was certainly God's Son" (Matthew 27:54).

Throughout this text, other questions also raise the issue of Jesus' identity. Pilate asked the crowds whether he should release a prisoner named Barabbas "or Jesus who is called Christ" (verse 17). When the crowds called for the release of Barabbas, Pilate responded, "Then what should I do with Jesus who is called Christ?" (verse 22). While Jesus suffered the pain and indignity of crucifixion, passersby asked, "So you were going to destroy the temple and rebuild it in three days, were you?" (verse 40). Even Jesus' cry from the cross took the form of a question: "My God, my God, why have you left me?" (verse 46). In their own way, each of these questions asks, who is this Jesus? Is he simply *called* "Christ," or is he truly the Messiah, the anointed One of God? Is he able to destroy and rebuild a temple in three days? Is he just one more prisoner crucified among many, forgotten and forsaken by God?

In spite of the sign confirming Jesus' identity as the King of the Jews, in spite of the centurion's testimony to Jesus as the Son of God, for the most part these questions are left unanswered in our text, for it ends on Good Friday with the death of Jesus. Later in Matthew 27, one of his disciples, the wealthy Joseph of Arimathea, would ask for Jesus' body and lay it in his own tomb with a large stone covering the entrance. Fearing that Jesus' disciples might later steal the body and claim that he had risen from the dead, some of the chief priests and Pharisees insisted that the grave be sealed. Pilate gave them permission to post a guard at the tomb to keep watch (Matthew 27:57-66).

Like the suffering servant of Isaiah 50, Jesus did nothing to prevent his fate. He did not argue with his accusers. He did not retaliate against those who beat him and crucified him. Instead, he responded with few words, a lot of silence, much suffering, agonizing prayer, and steadfast endurance to the end. He allowed his righteousness to speak for itself, as it did to Pilate's wife in her dream (Matthew 27:19). He allowed others to supply the testimony to his identity. In the face of injustice, he relied on God's justice in God's time. In the face of scorn, he refused to stoop to the same level of contempt. In the face of violence, he chose a path of nonviolence.

Today some argue that nonviolence simply doesn't work—it can't bring back kidnapped schoolgirls, prevent child soldiers, stop suicide bombers, or end wars. What are words, silence, prayer, and other nonviolent strategies in the face of such complex national and international problems, or even on a community or personal level? After all, Jesus' own nonviolent response ended with his suffering and death. Those who taunted him proved to be right; Jesus didn't save himself from the cross. Instead, he chose to save the world.

Three days later, on Easter Sunday morning, God's answer to all of the questions about Jesus came in the resurrection. Yes, Jesus is the Christ, the Messiah and Anointed One of God. Yes, the temple of Jesus' body had been beaten and broken, but gained new life on the third day. Yes, Jesus is God's Son, not at all forgotten or forsaken, but fully vindicated in his passion and in his rising again. Our text ends with Jesus' passion on Good Friday, but Resurrection Sunday is coming! ━

How do you feel as you read Matthew's account of Jesus' passion? Pained by the cruelty? angry at the injustice? in awe like the centurion? something else? How will you best express those feelings?

Psalm 31:9-16

9 Have mercy on me, LORD, because I'm depressed.
   My vision fails because of my grief,
   as do my spirit and my body.
10 My life is consumed with sadness;
   my years are consumed with groaning.
 Strength fails me because of my suffering;
   my bones dry up.
11 I'm a joke to all my enemies,
   still worse to my neighbors.
   I scare my friends,
   and whoever sees me in the street runs away!
12 I am forgotten, like I'm dead,
   completely out of mind;
   I am like a piece of pottery, destroyed.
13 Yes, I've heard all the gossiping,
   terror all around;
 so many gang up together against me,
   they plan to take my life!
14 But me? I trust you, LORD!
   I affirm, "You are my God."
15 My future is in your hands.
   Don't hand me over to my enemies,
   to all who are out to get me!
16 Shine your face on your servant;
   save me by your faithful love!

GROUP STUDY GUIDE

Questions for Discussion

1. Are you more familiar with Palm Sunday or Passion Sunday? How might emphasizing one and/or the other shape the life of your congregation and you personally?

2. In Isaiah 50:9, the suffering servant says, "Look! The Lord God will help me. Who will condemn me?" Reread Matthew 27:11-54. Who condemns Jesus? In what way does God help him?

3. In the ancient world, names conveyed the character and significance of a person or place. So when our text from Philippians speaks of the name of Jesus, it carries the full weight of his identity. What does it mean for you to "confess that Jesus Christ is Lord"? How do you express that by your words and actions?

4. Psalm 31:9-16 speaks of suffering, which could be related to depression. List all of the symptoms mentioned in these few verses. What gives the psalmist comfort in the midst of this experience? How have mental health issues impacted you and your family?

5. If you chose to give up something for Lent, how are you doing with your practice? Has it served to remind you of Jesus' sacrifice? In what way has it deepened your experience or understanding of self-sacrifice?

Suggestions for Group Study

Pray for Those Suffering Injustice

Page through a newspaper or scroll through an online news feed to identify areas of injustice in the world, such as people who have been attacked or people who are on the margins. Who makes the headlines? Who receives much less attention? Who is missing? Pray in your own words for those who are suffering, or use the following template:

O God of the suffering servant, and the Helper of all who call on your name, we pray for the people and places who are suffering today and name them before you:_____
_____. We remember especially those who may feel forgotten:_____. We pray for the suffering in our own lives. [moment of silence] Guide our steps, that we might discern when to speak and when to be silent, when to act and when to wait. We place our trust in you. Amen.

Debate Nonviolence

Nonviolence is sometimes criticized as passive or ineffective. But Jesus' active nonviolence confirmed his identity, led to his resurrection, and ushered in a new era of the church as his body on earth and a signpost of God's kingdom. Throughout history, nonviolent action has also played a role in the political independence of India, the anti-apartheid struggle in South Africa, the civil rights movement in the United States, and the dismantling of other injustice around the world. Form two groups and have a debate, with one side speaking in favor of nonviolence and the other speaking against. What evidence and examples can you present? Are you more comfortable speaking for one side or the other? In what way(s) can you see yourself following Jesus' example of nonviolence?

Closing Prayer

The ancient world didn't know what to do with you, Lord Jesus. As itinerant preacher and teacher, visionary and healer, the one who upset the establishment in favor of God's kingdom, you challenged the political, social, and religious powers by your life and teaching.

Your death literally shook the world. Your Resurrection three days later changed history and changes our lives today. The world still doesn't know what to do with you, Lord Jesus. But the bigger question is, what will you do with us? Be our guide as we seek to follow you. Be our word when we are weary, our helper in times of trouble, our Savior who holds us close. Grant us humility and hope, and fill us with the power of your Resurrection. Amen.

Tributes to Christ Jesus

Scriptures for Easter
Acts 10:34-43
Colossians 3:1-4
Matthew 28:1-10

One year for our Good Friday worship, we held a funeral for Jesus that included his life story from birth to death, tributes by young adults representing Peter and Mary Magdalene, and a present-day tribute to Jesus shared by one of our newer church members. Then I invited everyone in the congregation to write their own tribute to Jesus and place it on a large cross at the front of the church.

With their permission, I selected several to share as part of our Easter Sunday worship. Some of the tributes were just one line: "Jesus teaches me what it means to love others." Others said more: "Jesus, the only Friend who is always there for me, the only friend I can trust completely. He has made all the difference in my life."

Each of the Scripture readings for this week might be understood as a kind of tribute or testimony to Christ Jesus. Apart from the Psalm, each text comes from the New Testament, with Acts 10:34-43 standing in for the usual Old Testament text. In it, Jesus' closest friend and disciple, Simon Peter, delivers a classic three-point sermon centered on Jesus' life, death, and resurrection. He ends with the ringing tribute that "everyone who believes in him receives forgiveness of sins through his name" (Acts 10:43).

The Gospel text recounts that first Easter morning when Mary Magdalene and another Mary go to the tomb, and instead of finding Jesus' body, they find the tomb empty. An angel tells them that Jesus has risen from the dead! As they hurry back to tell the other disciples, the two women actually meet Jesus on the way, and they fall at his feet to worship him. Their tribute of worship expresses both their joy at seeing him alive and their awe at what God has done.

In the Epistle text, attention focuses on the risen Christ and the implications of the Resurrection for the first readers of Colossians and for us today. The human-divine Jesus, who announced the kingdom of God and gave up his life, now reigns as the risen Christ with God in divine glory. In Jesus Christ, we too have died and gained new life. So we offer the tribute of our lives, looking beyond the earthiness of "anger, rage, malice, slander, and obscene language" (Colossians 3:8) to "put on compassion, kindness, humility, gentleness, and patience" (Colossians 3:12).

These three texts amply demonstrate the testimony of the psalm: "I won't die—no, I will live and declare what the Lord has done. . . . This is the day the Lord acted; we will rejoice and celebrate in it!" (Psalm 118:17, 24). Writing centuries earlier, the psalmist had no knowledge of what was to come, but the faithful love of God extolled in his psalm would one day be revealed even more fully in the life, death, and resurrection of Jesus. As the psalmist writes, "The stone rejected by the builders is now the main foundation stone!" (Psalm 118:22). In the Gospel accounts, Jesus applies these words to himself, so angering the religious leaders that they wanted him arrested (Mark 12:1-12; Matthew 21:33-46; Luke 20:9-19). When Peter is later arrested for teaching about Jesus' resurrection, he makes the same reference to these words in his testimony before the elders and other leaders of the people (Acts 4:11), and refers to them again in a letter to churches (1 Peter 2:4-8). The words of the psalmist written long ago became a fitting tribute to the crucified and risen Christ.

EASTER IS FOR EVERYONE
ACTS 10:34-43

Our local newspaper carried an ad with a furry, fuzzy toy rabbit wearing a jacket and carrying a basket of Easter eggs. "Has the true meaning of Easter gotten a little fuzzy?" said the caption. Then in slightly smaller print, "Give your children more than bunnies and baskets this year. Give them a miracle. Join us on Easter as we celebrate the resurrection of Jesus Christ."

The message in our text from Acts is anything but fuzzy. Peter had been one of Jesus' closest followers, and in our text he delivers a powerful sermon that could well have been titled "Easter is for Everyone." But instead of facing a congregation from the pulpit on an Easter Sunday morning, Peter speaks more informally in the home of Cornelius, a Roman centurion who is also a devout and God-fearing man (Acts 10:1-2). One afternoon, as Cornelius had been praying, an angel came to him in a vision and told him to send for Simon Peter and listen to him. Cornelius follows the angel's instructions, and by the time Peter arrives, Cornelius has gathered a whole houseful of people.

What an unlikely pair—Peter, a Jew whose religious tradition prevents him from associating with outsiders, and Cornelius, a Roman centurion who is the very definition of a Jewish outsider. God is clearly doing something new as Peter, a follower of Jesus, the Prince of Peace, meets with Cornelius, a member and officer of the Italian Company. The two men wouldn't normally tolerate coming together under the same roof, yet here Peter arrives as an invited guest, and Cornelius waits eagerly to hear what Peter has to say. No one is more surprised at this unlikely gathering than Peter himself, and so he begins with a startling confession: "I really am learning that God doesn't show partiality to one group of people over another" (verse 34). What Peter has to say is for everyone.

Peter's address begins with his main point: Jesus Christ is Lord of all (verse 36). Not only Lord of the Jews as represented by Peter himself. Not only Lord of the Gentiles as represented by Cornelius. But Lord of all—Jew and Gentile, fisherman and soldier, men and women, older and younger, rich and poor, married and single, whatever stage or station of life. Jesus Christ is Lord of all! Then Peter goes on to support this bold assertion with three lines of evidence, three essential things to know about Jesus.

First, Jesus spent his life doing good. Peter specifically mentions healing, but from the Gospel accounts we know that Jesus also engaged in preaching, teaching, mentoring his disciples, reaching out to the poor and marginalized, feeding the hungry, comforting the grief-stricken, challenging the religious and political establishment of his day, and even raising people from the dead. Just as Peter notes that God does not show partiality to one group over another, so Jesus demonstrated that same quality in his good works. He treated the Samaritan woman at the well (John 4:5-42) with the same respect that he showed to Nicodemus as a Jewish leader (John 3:1-21). He raised a young girl from the dead (Luke 8:40-56) and similarly gave new life to a young man (Luke 7:11-15). He fed the crowds of men, women, and children (Matthew 15:32-39). He healed the daughter of a Syrophoenician woman (Mark 7:24-30), a Roman centurion's servant (Luke 7:1-10), and a Jewish-Samaritan group of men suffering from leprosy (Luke 17:11-19). In all these good works done freely and without partiality, Jesus relied on the power of God who anointed him with the Holy Spirit.

In Peter's sermon, the second essential thing to know about Jesus is that "they killed him by hanging him on a tree" (verse 39). In other words, Jesus died by crucifixion, a particularly cruel form of capital punishment which meant being nailed or tied to a cross and left to die. Crucifixion generally meant a slow and painful death, the punishment for traitors and murderers. But Jesus did not die trying to overthrow the government; instead, he insisted that his kingdom was not of this world (John 18:36). He did not die as a murderer; in fact, Jesus refused to use violence even to defend himself (Luke 22:47-53) and taught his followers to pray for their enemies (Matthew 5:43-44). Jesus did not die for his own wrongdoing or guilt, but for the sake of others, "to serve and to give his life to liberate many people" (Mark 10:45).

So Jesus spent his life doing good, and he died on the cross for the sake of others. And the third essential thing to know about Jesus is that on the third day after his death, he rose again to new life. No one actually saw God's act of Resurrection, but many people saw Jesus alive after the fact, including Peter. He along with Thomas, Nathanael, and some of Jesus' other disciples even had breakfast with Jesus one morning (John 21:1-14). So they knew that Jesus was truly alive. He had gained the victory over the powers that put him to death. And we know that today in the same way that we know of any other event in history: by the testimony of eyewitnesses who shared the good news, by those who wrote it down and who passed it on over the years.

Today, many people accept that Jesus lived a good life, that he was a great teacher. Many accept that he died by crucifixion. A person who lived the way he did was bound to get into trouble. If Jesus simply lived and died like everyone else, then maybe it would be enough to think of him in that way—as a good man, as a great teacher, even as a miracle worker. After all, there have been many other great teachers in history, many others who have allowed themselves to be martyred for a cause beyond themselves.

But the resurrection of Jesus means that he was not only a good person, a great teacher, and a miracle worker, but the risen Christ who is Lord of all—Lord of all people and powers, Lord even over sin and death. In this life, sin still hurts us, and when we sin we hurt others and need to face the consequences. But the resurrection of Jesus means that sin has already been defeated. We have forgiveness with God. Death still stings, and the pain we feel at the death of a loved one may remain with us in some form for the rest of our lives. But the resurrection of Jesus means that death has already been defeated. In Jesus Christ, we have the hope of resurrection and eternal life.

For some, this is an old, familiar message. As Peter says at the start of his sermon, "You know what happened. . . . You know about Jesus of Nazareth" (verses 37, 38). For others, the significance of Jesus' life, death, and resurrection may be a new thought. Either way, Peter's message comes across clearly: Jesus lived, died, and rose again by the power of God. Easter is for everyone.

How have you celebrated Easter as a child, young person, and adult? In what ways do your celebrations reflect the central message of Easter as presented in Peter's sermon? In what ways are they simply fun?

LIFE WITH CHRIST
COLOSSIANS 3:1-4

"Jesus has an identity crisis," read the cover of a news magazine. Is he a regular guy? the article asked. Or is he a vengeful prophet? A political activist? A rabbi, or perhaps a company man? Son of God? Street preacher? Revolutionary? Different pictures seem to emerge depending on whom you ask, and some even suggest that perhaps the church no longer needs Jesus. After all, we have activists and inspiring personalities of our own day, so why look to a long-ago figure for inspiration and religious teaching? Who is Jesus?

According to the four Gospels, in some ways Jesus *was* a regular guy who ate with his friends and got tired, hungry, and thirsty just like we do. He lived as an itinerant preacher and teacher, as a miracle worker who relieved suffering by healing the sick and even raising the dead, as a prophet who predicted his own death and resurrection. In his hometown, people wondered at his teaching, and asked, "Isn't this the carpenter? Isn't he Mary's son and the brother of James, Joses, Judas, and Simon? Aren't his sisters here with us? (Mark 6:3). When Jesus asked his disciples, "Who do people say that I am?" they responded, "Some say John the Baptist, others Elijah, and still others one of the prophets" (Mark 8:27-28).

Colossians 3 brings attention to Jesus' identity in yet another way, not with questions but with a clear focus on the risen Christ. Our text shifts the focus from Jesus' earthly life to his identity as Jesus Christ, the resurrected Son of God. Suffering and death could not keep him down. Sin and evil could not contain him. Instead, God performed a new and mighty miracle by raising him from the dead. The resurrection of Jesus declared God's resounding yes to his life and ministry. It vindicated all that Jesus taught and all that he stood for. Love God. Love your neighbor. Love your enemy. Christ is alive!

The death and resurrection of Jesus has profound implications for all those who follow him. According to our text, we are joined to Christ in his death and resurrection. Our life is "hidden" with Christ—not in the sense of being hidden away from prying eyes, but the force of the original Greek word conveys a sense of being shielded and kept safe. When Christ is revealed, we too shall be revealed in glory. To some this may sound like impossible science fiction, to others religious mysticism, but this theological understanding of our union with Christ is meant to be lived out in the real world by real people.

Because our life is now with Christ, we are to "think about the things above and not things on earth" (verse 2). Our text uses metaphorical language to contrast two ways of being—not literally meaning above and below, but the life of the risen Christ in contrast to life without him. The verses that follow our text more fully describe what this means. The things "above" include "compassion, kindness, humility, gentleness, and patience" (verse 12), while the things "on earth" include "anger, rage, malice, slander, and obscene language" (verse 8). The things of earth have already died with our old life, and because Christ is alive, because now we live in him, we live a new Christ-like life.

For one of my baptism and church membership classes, I asked: How do you expect a Christian to behave? Should we be able to tell a Christian by their actions? What is their identity? As the group called out their ideas, I wrote them on the markerboard: honest, generous, kind, church-going, loving, accepting of other people, prayerful, giving, serving/volunteering, being a good neighbor. Some in the class were relatively new to Christian faith and to the church, while others were part of our leadership team helping with the class. Together, they came up with a list of qualities that reflected their understanding of Christian behavior. We didn't read Colossians that day, but their list reflected the same understanding that Christian identity results in Christian behavior. Because of Christ, we live a Christ-like life.

A friend tells me that one day she was riding on a city bus that came to a stop at a busy intersection. A passenger who was obviously drunk got off the bus, but wasn't able to cross the street with so much traffic. As the bus continued to wait at the stop, the other passengers sat waiting and watching, until finally another woman stood up and said in a loud voice, "And I call myself a Christian?!" With that, she got off the bus, helped the man across the street, then returned and took her seat. "That might not have been the safest, smartest thing to do," says my friend, "and fortunately the bus didn't leave until she got back. But I've never forgotten what she said: 'And I call myself a Christian?!'" Because of Christ, we live a Christ-like life.

Yet for every positive example of Christian identity and behavior, I can think of other examples where Christians have apparently failed to live out our identity in Christ. We have not always left behind the anger, malice, selfishness and other things of this earth. We are not always compassionate, kind, humble, honest, and neighborly as we know we ought to be. All too easily we slip back to take up the things of earth instead of living out our new identity in Christ. It is not Jesus with the identity crisis, but us.

In our Epistle text, the solution to our identity crisis lies in the reminder that Christ *is* our life. We have died and risen with him, and will one day share his glory. In the meantime, our life is safe with him. We have a new identity in Christ Jesus—now we need to act like it.

Do you think the woman who got off the bus to help the man cross the street did the right thing? What would you have done in her place?

SEARCHING FOR JESUS
MATTHEW 28:1-10

A pastor friend of mine has always been puzzled by the various accounts of Jesus' resurrection in the four Gospels. Why, for example, does Mary Magdalene appear to be at Jesus' tomb by herself in John's Gospel (John 20:11-18), but here in Matthew's account, Mary Magdalene comes to the tomb with "the other Mary" (Matthew 28:1)? Why does Mary say, "I've seen the Lord" (John 20:18) in one account, when that line is missing from the others? So this year, my friend worked through all four Gospel accounts to piece together his own timeline with all of the details from that first Easter morning.

While I appreciate his effort to build a comprehensive timeline, for the most part I'm content to let each Gospel speak for itself with its own unique voice and emphasis. It's like when my three sisters and I get together. Although we grew up in the same household and share some of the same experiences, when we talk about them later, our versions sometimes sound quite different. I usually remember more about who was there and what they said. Another of my sisters might remember what people wore, and another would have the pictures to prove it. We retell the same story in different ways because we're each unique, and we find different things significant. So too with the four Gospel writers as they highlight different details and different parts of the same story. But in each retelling, the basic message remains the same: after an exemplary life, Jesus died on the cross, he was buried, and three days later, by the power of God, he rose again to new life.

In our Gospel text, Matthew seems to emphasize the visual. So he describes the angel's appearance with a face "like lightning" and dressed in clothes "as white as snow" (verse 3), and he repeatedly uses verbs of seeing and looking. The two Marys came "to *look*" at the tomb (verse 1); "*Look*, there was a great earthquake" (verse 2); the angel said "I know that you are *looking* for Jesus. . . Come, *see* the place where they laid him. . . . You will *see* him" (verses 5-7); and Jesus says in the final verse, "Go and tell my brothers that I am going into Galilee. They will *see* me there" (verse 10, emphasis added).

These verbs highlight the physical nature of Jesus' resurrection. The angel says that the women will see Jesus, and they do physically see him on their way back from the tomb. They don't imagine him in a common dream. They don't see a ghost. When the women meet Jesus on the way, they fall to the ground and take hold of his feet (verse 9). Later, he would walk on the road to Emmaus with two of his disciples and break bread with them (Luke 24:13-32). He would have breakfast on the beach with Simon Peter and some of the other disciples (John 21:9-14). Jesus rose from the dead with a real body that others could see.

At the same time, the verbs of looking and seeing stand metaphorically for a different kind of seeing with the eyes of the heart. While the Gospel text says that the women came to look at the tomb, the angel knew that they were really looking for Jesus, their friend and teacher. Much like we might visit a graveside today, most often we don't go only to see the physical grave, to make sure that we remember where it is, to see that it's well kept and to bring fresh flowers. Beyond those practical, physical reasons, we go to the graveside to grieve, to remember, to seek comfort, to feel a connection again with our loved one who has died. So, too, as the two Marys went looking for the tomb, we might imagine them in their heart of hearts looking for Jesus.

When the women arrived at the tomb, the text says that the angel rolled away the stone. In the Gospel of John, when Jesus went to raise his friend, Lazarus, the stone covering the entrance to Lazarus' tomb was also rolled away. In that case, the stone was rolled away so that Lazarus could come out of the tomb (John 11:38-44). But with the resurrection of Jesus, the angel didn't roll away the stone to let Jesus out—Jesus had already risen. He was already out of the tomb. The resurrected Christ Jesus didn't need anyone to remove the stone to let him out, just as he didn't need anyone to open the door when he later appeared to his disciples in a locked room (John 20:26). Instead, the angel rolled away the stone so the women could see in.

At that moment, everything changed. Whatever sorrow, confusion, and worry the women may have had on their way to the tomb gave way to a new kind of fear and excitement (verse 8). How fearsome and yet how joyous—Jesus was alive! They now had a new purpose to go and tell the other disciples. And when they met Jesus on their way, they fell at his feet to worship him.

Today, we may have our own sorrows, confusion, and worry. We may feel overwhelmed by life and its pressures. There is plenty to fear and mourn in this world of hunger and hurt, distress, destruction, and death. But the resurrection of Jesus gives us a vision beyond this flawed and fragile life. The brokenness and grief of this world can be transformed. Because of Jesus risen from the dead, we may be afraid yet filled with joy. Like the two Marys, we receive a new purpose to spread the good news and a new reason to worship.

What boulders stand in our way to prevent us from seeing and experiencing Christ's resurrection in this way? Some may be troubled by the apparent differences in the Bible. Some may be preoccupied with the challenges of daily living—just getting up in the morning and making it to the end of the day with yourself and your family intact can be a major challenge. Others may feel distracted by the spirit of our age that seems to flit restlessly from one political argument to another, from one religious controversy to another. But the empty tomb announces the reality of God's resurrection that surpasses all of these things. The stone has rolled away, Jesus is alive, and we are empowered with new life by his Spirit.

What boulders stand in your way to prevent you from seeing and experiencing Christ's resurrection? Who in your life is like the angel removing the barriers so you can see?

Psalm 118:1-2, 14-24

¹ Give thanks to the LORD because he is good,
　　because his faithful love lasts forever.
² Let Israel say it:
　　"God's faithful love lasts forever!"

¹⁴ The LORD was my strength and protection;
　　he was my saving help!
¹⁵ The sounds of joyful songs and deliverance
　　are heard in the tents of the righteous:
　　"The LORD's strong hand is victorious!
¹⁶ The LORD's strong hand is ready to strike!
　　The LORD's strong hand is victorious!"
¹⁷ I won't die—no, I will live
　　and declare what the LORD has done.
¹⁸ Yes, the LORD definitely disciplined me,
　　but he didn't hand me over to death.
¹⁹ Open the gates of righteousness for me
　　so I can come in and give thanks to the LORD!
²⁰ This is the LORD's gate;
　　those who are righteous enter through it.
²¹ I thank you because you answered me,
　　because you were my saving help.
²² The stone rejected by the builders
　　is now the main foundation stone!
²³ This has happened because of the LORD;
　　it is astounding in our sight!
²⁴ This is the day the LORD acted;
　　we will rejoice and celebrate in it!

GROUP STUDY GUIDE

Questions for Discussion

1. In Acts 10:1-16, Cornelius and Peter each receive a vision from God that leads to their remarkable meeting in our Acts text. In Cornelius' vision, an angel directs him to send for Peter (verses 3-6); in Peter's vision, God shows him that Jews and Gentiles can come together (verses 10-16, 28). For both, the visions took place during a time of prayer, and both acted on the message they received from God. How has God spoken to you in prayer, and how have you responded? Have you ever received a vision or dream from God?

2. Peter ends his sermon in Acts 10 with the forgiveness of sins (verse 43). Yet in our own day, in society at large and even in the church, there seems to be a de-emphasis on sin and forgiveness. Do you sense that too? Is Peter's emphasis still relevant today? And if so, how might it best be communicated?

3. Our Colossians text speaks quite generally of the things of "earth" and the things "above." Read through the verses that immediately follow, Colossians 3:5-17, for further details. Then use a markerboard to list the things of earth in one column and things above in another. On the basis of verse 17, what else would you add to the list of things above? In what ways do you live out this identity in Christ? What prevents you from living more fully into this new life?

4. In Matthew 28, the two Marys leave the tomb with a new purpose to tell Jesus' disciples about his resurrection (verse 7, compare verse 10). Jesus' words to "go and tell" foreshadow the broader commission he gives at the end of Matthew's Gospel to go and make disciples of all nations (Matthew 28:19-20). As the women go, they meet Jesus, fall down to worship him, and clasp his feet. The original Greek here means to hold on strongly to something, to hold on and not let go. So in this text, the women respond to Jesus' resurrection with both mission and worship, with both sharing the good news and fervent worship. How can we hold mission and worship together today without emphasizing one at the expense of the other?

5. If you gave up something for Lent, do you feel like indulging in it now? Would that be a fitting celebration for Easter? Why or why not?

Suggestions for Group Study

Write a Tribute to Jesus

Write your own tribute to Jesus that expresses what he means to you. Consider both his earthly life and ministry, and his identity and power as the risen Christ. How have you been impacted by the earthly Jesus? How has the risen Christ been active in your life? Give an opportunity for sharing your tributes as a group, and consider sharing them in worship or in your church newsletter.

Reflect on New Life and Give Thanks to God

In the history of the Christian church, Easter has been observed not only as a day of celebration, but as a season lasting 50 days from Easter Sunday to Pentecost. During this season, the royal purple of Lent gives way to white as the liturgical color which symbolizes the sinless, holy Jesus and the bright light of his resurrection. Encourage everyone in your group in advance to wear something white to celebrate this new season. Light candles. Reflect on signs of new life and give thanks to God in one or more of the following ways, depending on the needs and personalities of your group:

- Allow time for personal reflection and journaling with or without music. Write a gratitude list, draw signs of new life, doodle the Psalm or other Scripture for this week, fold a paper airplane, or come up with your own expression of joy and celebration.
- Form a gratitude circle by joining hands and having each person express their thanks to God.
- Ask people in advance to bring a selection of personal photos, magazines, markers, and other items to create a collage as a group project. Choose a theme drawn from one of the Scripture readings for this week: new life in Christ, resurrection, worship, light.
- Come up with your own idea.

Closing Prayer

Lord Jesus Christ who lived, died, and rose again, we know that questions abound about who you are, about who God is, and about what it means to be Christian. We live with those questions too. Yet we know from Scripture that you now reign with God and are present with us by your Spirit. Grant us joy and confidence in the forgiveness and new life you offer. Where uncertainty or doubt linger, may we receive your reassurance and grow in faith. Where tears and distress pour forth, may your comfort and strength form a shield of protection. So may we live in the power of your resurrection, by your Spirit that gives us a new identity in you. Amen.